Tolley's
Guide to Self-Ass
for
Employers and Employees

by

Peter Gravestock FCA FTII ATT

Tolley Publishing Company Limited

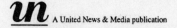 A United News & Media publication

Published by
Tolley Publishing Company Ltd
Tolley House
2 Addiscombe Road
Croydon, Surrey CR9 5AF England
0181-686 9141

Printed and bound in Great Britain by
Hobbs the Printers, Southampton

ISBN 1 86012 033-4

Preface

The reform of the personal taxation system in this country, by a gradual move to a system of self-assessment and a current year basis of assessment, has been discussed for a number of years. The first document forming the consultation process for the current changes was published in 1991.

The Finance Act 1994 introduced the first (albeit the major) tranche of legislation which, when completed, will encompass the whole personal taxation system, including employees as well as the self-employed.

The process has continued with the additional legislation contained in the Finance Act 1995, and further legislation must be expected as consultation takes place on the effect of these reforms on the taxpayer and the Revenue.

The result of these changes will be a complete change of emphasis such that the responsibility for all day-to-day actions relating to personal taxation falls upon the taxpayer, and the enforcement powers of the taxation authorities are significantly increased.

Peter Gravestock, FCA FTII ATT
Gravestock and Owen
Willenhall
West Midlands
October 1995

Contents

Contents

Chapter 1

Introduction

1.1   Income tax was originally introduced by Pitt. This was in an hour long Budget speech on 3 December 1798. The measure was unpopular and yielded a small amount of money, under £6 million in the first year. By 1801 the yield had fallen to under £5 million and in April 1802 Addington repealed the original income tax.

The abolition lasted as long as the peace with France and when hostilities recommenced in May 1803 the Budget of that year introduced what was called 'a separate tax on property'. Although passed under the title *Property Duty Act*, it was in fact income tax in another form and laid the foundation of the Schedular system. Despite a second abolition in 1816 income tax was reintroduced in the 1842 Budget and has been with us ever since. Many of the basic principles established in those early years are still with us today.

1.2   Before 1944 the yield from employees was comparatively low. This was due in part to a system that required tax to be paid twice yearly by the employed person. Accordingly, the PAYE system was introduced by the *Income Tax (Employments) Act 1943* with effect from 1944/45. The yield almost doubled following the introduction of PAYE. The system did not require the employee to make direct payments to the Revenue but imposed the obligation upon the employer to deduct tax at source. As a result, for the vast majority of taxpayers it was no longer necessary to file a completed tax return each year.

1.3   With the increased pressure upon the Government to be more efficient, it has not gone unnoticed that in the USA the same number of Revenue Officers collect many times the amount of tax collected in the UK from three times as many people. This is despite the requirement of all taxpayers to file a tax return.

The intention of the introduction of self-assessment is to retain the benefits of the PAYE system (i.e. deduction of tax at source from employed persons and the ability to collect tax without completed tax returns from each citizen), coupled with the advantages of the systems used in many other countries whereby the calculation of any additional tax due, over that deducted at source, is the responsibility of the taxpayer.

With effect from 6 April 1996 each taxpayer in the UK becomes responsible for his own tax assessing. However, because of the PAYE system the majority of employees will still not need to file a tax return each year. Furthermore, the Inland Revenue will continue to code in small adjustments, up to £1,000 per annum, by way of code number adjustments.

1.4   To achieve the benefits of self-assessment whilst retaining the benefits of PAYE, it has been necessary to amend the requirements of provision of information by employers. The changes are detailed in the following chapters.

1.5   Although the PAYE system will collect the correct amount of tax from most employees it will be the responsibility of each and every taxpayer to ask for a tax return if he has a liability to tax on income that is not taxed at source, or a liability to higher rate tax from income other than employment. In addition, new sources of income must be notified to the Revenue against a strict time limit, and for the first time there is a statutory requirement to maintain the records needed for the completion of a tax return. Any taxpayer receiving a tax return will be obliged to compute his liability to tax by 31 January following the end of the fiscal year (or three months after receipt of a tax return if later), or to submit the return to the Revenue by 30 September following the end of the tax year (or two months after receipt of tax return if later) in order that the Revenue may compute the tax due on behalf of the taxpayer. It is expected that approximately four million employed persons will receive tax returns each year. This will include directors, employees liable to higher rate tax and others to whom tax returns are sent.

Everyone who gets a tax return will need to enter figures for income, gains, reliefs and deductions. For employed persons this means that they will no longer be able to write 'per PAYE' or 'per P11D' on the returns.

To complete a tax return will require the employee to keep all paperwork relating to employment as well as documents relating to any other income. This will include all coding notices relating to the year, P45 (copy 1A) on change of employment, P60 at the year end and copies of forms P11D or P9D. Employees will also need to keep details of all other income received including dividend vouchers, certificate of tax deducted on bank and building society interest and records of all other income received.

1.6   The new regime moves the responsibility for the computation of the correct tax liability from the Inland Revenue to the employee. However, the operation of the PAYE system will mean that the vast majority of employees will notice no change to the tax system other than when they receive a revised income tax form for completion. Most employees will, however, receive more documents from their employer relating to their tax affairs which they will be obliged to keep, together with the code notices issued by the Inland Revenue.

1.7   The above measures are considered in detail in the following chapters. As this is a new system it must be expected that further legislation will be required and it is known that a number of measures will be introduced in the *Finance Act 1996*. In practical terms it will also be possible for changes to be introduced in the *Finance Act 1997*. Care should be taken to incorporate such later legislation into the measures described in this book.

Chapter 2

Self-Assessment

The present procedure

2.1 The UK tax system has been based upon the premise that the Inland Revenue assesses the taxpayer. There is an obligation for the taxpayer to report to the Revenue sources of income, and the Revenue will normally issue a tax return on which the quantum of income can be declared to the Inland Revenue source by source. Having received such information, the Revenue will assess the taxpayer. It is the duty of the Inspector to raise the assessment based upon the details of income provided to him, but if it appears to him that the return is incomplete or incorrect or has not been made, then he may assess income tax to the best of his judgement.

Income in the UK is computed for taxation purposes by reference to the Schedular system. The relevant tax office issues assessments for income source by source, the tax return being submitted to the taxpayer's main taxing district which co-ordinates the issuing of assessments and the granting of allowances. If the Revenue does not make an assessment on returned income then there is no liability to tax. When an assessment is made, the taxpayer may appeal against the assessment and the final assessable profits will be determined by agreement, pending appeal, or by the appeals procedure.

If the Inland Revenue has raised an assessment which the taxpayer believes to be excessive, the remedy is to appeal. At that time it is possible to make a separate postponement application to hold-over the tax believed to be excessive. If such a postponement application is accepted by the Revenue, then the taxpayer is only obliged to pay the agreed reduced tax, and interest, if any, will only be charged on the balance of the tax liability.

Once an assessment has been agreed it cannot be changed. However, the taxpayer may make an error or mistake claim if he discovers that the assessment is incorrect. The Revenue may issue a further assessment if the Inspector discovers that profits have not been assessed, or that the assessment has become insufficient. The assessment cannot be amended merely because the Inspector of Taxes has failed to act upon the information available to him (*Scorer v Olin Energy Systems Limited 1985 STC 218*).

Where the taxpayer is employed then a tax return is only issued to an employee infrequently. However, if a taxpayer has a new source of income, or becomes a higher rate taxpayer, or makes a capital gain then he must request a tax return. The new source of income or gain must be notified to the Revenue within one year of the end of the fiscal year in which it arises.

Tax is collected from employees primarily by way of the PAYE system. Normal liabilities to tax including those arising on benefits in kind, e.g. cars will be collected by way of code number adjustments. If the liability exceeds the available allowances then the code number is prefixed by a letter K indicating that the amount should be added to the taxable income, rather than that the allowances should be deducted from the taxable income. The maximum tax deductible under the 'K' code system is 50% of the gross earnings for any period.

Because of the PAYE system the Inland Revenue does not have to issue assessments to the majority of taxpayers each year. However, an assessment will be issued to any employed taxpayer on request. If any assessment is issued showing an underpayment then the Revenue will normally code the underpayment into the coding notice of the next complete fiscal year, e.g. if the Revenue issues an assessment in December 1995 then the code number to be adjusted would be that of 1996/97. If the Revenue becomes aware of the need to adjust the coding notice during the fiscal year, e.g. when a company car is changed giving rise to a higher benefit then it will adjust the benefit immediately issuing a new coding notice on a week 1 or month 1 basis. This means that the new notice will apply from that time forward but will not be adjusted on the cumulative income to the date of the issue of the notice. As a result an underpayment for the current year can become apparent to the Revenue during the tax year. Such an underpayment is coded into the next fiscal year's coding notice, e.g. in November 1995 the Revenue issues a month 1 coding notice to a taxpayer having been notified that his motor vehicle had changed in July 1995. (The information will be made available to the Revenue by the completion by the employer of form P46(car) which has to be filed within 28 days from the end of the quarter in which the change took place.) For a change of motor vehicle in July 1995 this would require form P46(car) being filed within 28 days after 5 October 1995. The

Revenue can then adjust the coding notice from December forward, but the underpayment arising between July and November will not be collected at that time. The calculated underpayment would then be adjusted upon the 1996/97 code notice. Note that in this instance the underpayment is collected in the following year whereas the assessment issued in December 1995 above would be for the year 1994/95. The underpayment then collected in 1996/97 would be 2 years old.

When a taxpayer submits a tax return showing small amounts of other income, e.g. National Savings investment account interest, then the Revenue will often not issue an assessment but 'code in' the income. This again reduces the number of assessments issued to employed persons.

If the underpayment is large, e.g. in excess of £1,000 then it is Revenue policy to collect the same by way of direct assessment. The liability has to be paid 14 days after the Collector demands the amount due. This will be not less than 30 days after the issue of the assessment.

Self-assessment

2.2   From 1996/97 the long-established practice of the Inland Revenue assessing liabilities will cease. Instead the taxpayer will be responsible for insuring that his tax liabilities are computed and paid to the Revenue by the due date. To assist, the Inland Revenue will still complete the computation of tax liability providing the return is filed by 30 September following the year of assessment. Although the Revenue may be requested to compute the tax liability, it is still undertaking the task effectively as agent for the taxpayer and the resultant assessment is still known as a self-assessment. Accordingly, the onus of assessment moves from the Inland Revenue to the taxpayer.

If a taxpayer is prepared to compute his own tax liability then he need not file his tax return until 31 January following the end of the fiscal year. However, if the taxpayer wishes to have an underpayment coded in to his PAYE code number then he must file the tax return by **30 September** even if he has computed his own tax liability.

2.3   The new tax return will consist of a summary schedule together with personal details. If the taxpayer wishes to compute his own tax liability then he must also complete a schedule showing the amount to be paid. There will be separate schedules for certain types of income, capital gains and amounts relating to earlier years. In the main tax return all items will be shown for the actual fiscal year in question on a current year basis. The tax return is considered in greater detail in Chapter 10.

Administration

Payment dates

2.4   As a consequence of the new tax return and self-assessment provisions, the date of payment of income tax and capital gains tax alters. In the case of capital gains tax, the liability becomes due on 31 January following the end of the year of assessment.

For income tax, payments on account will normally be required. The actual tax liability of the preceding year will be used as the basis on the payments on account. The liability for this purpose will be the amount assessed in the preceding year, less amounts deducted at source, deductions under PAYE, SC60 tax paid, tax credits and notional tax credits. There will be no adjustment for changing levels of income or tax rates or allowances.

The effect of the new regime is that tax will be due half yearly on most types of income on which tax was previously payable by assessment. Previously income from land and from untaxed sources, e.g. interest received gross had been due on 1 January during the year of assessment. In the same way tax on income liable to higher rate tax had been payable on 1 December following the year of assessment. In future all of these sources of income will be payable as to:

(*a*)   one-half on 31 January during the tax year; and

(*b*)   one-half on 31 July following.

The payments on account will be 50% of the relevant figure. As set out above the relevant figure is the equivalent amount payable directly to the Revenue for the previous year.

When the actual tax liability for the year is computed the balance of tax payable, or repayable, will be due on 31 January following the end of the year of assessment.

There are provisions to enable a taxpayer to reduce the interim payments where it is believed that his liability for the current year will be less than in the previous year.

Interest will be charged on all late payments and repayments of interest will be paid on any overpayments from the due date, or the date of payment if later.

For further details see 2.21 below.

Enforcement

2.5 There will be automatic penalties for failure to file a tax return by the due date. Furthermore, any tax unpaid 28 days after the filing date for the tax return will be subject to a surcharge of 5%. That surcharge increases to 10% if the tax is unpaid six months after the relevant filing date. See Chapter 5.

Corrections to returns

2.6 Where a taxpayer does not have full information by the relevant filing date, he will be required to make a best estimate. Tax will be payable on that estimate. When the information is available to complete the return, interest will be charged on the tax due from the normal due date to the date of payment, or repayment interest paid on the tax repayable from the due date (or date of payment if later) to the date of repayment. Surcharges and penalties will not apply.

The taxpayer will be able to correct his tax return at any time in the period of twelve months from the normal filing date. The Revenue will be able to correct a tax return for obvious errors in a period of nine months from the date on which the return is actually filed. This process will be known as 'repairing' a tax return. For further details see 2.16 below.

Enquiries into a return

2.7 The Revenue will have the power to enquire into any tax return. If the Revenue wishes to exercise this power it must give notice in writing within one year of the filing date. This period is extended if the taxpayer is late in filing his tax return. After such a notice has been given, it will not be possible to repair a tax return.

The Revenue will be required to issue a formal notice when it has completed its enquiries. If a taxpayer believes that an enquiry should not have been undertaken, or is being continued unreasonably, he can ask the General Commissioners to issue a notice requiring the Revenue to close the enquiries. When the Revenue has completed its enquiries, it must issue a formal notice to the taxpayer. After such a notice has been issued, it will not be possible for the Revenue to conduct further enquiries into that tax return unless there is a discovery. See 2.17 below.

Determination of tax where no return delivered

2.8   If a taxpayer does not file his tax return then the Revenue will have powers to issue a determination. The tax shown on such a determination will be payable without appeal and no postponement of tax will be possible. The determination will be superseded when the tax return and self-assessment are filed.

Discovery

2.9   The legislation introduces provisions relating to discovery. In simple terms, a discovery assessment will only be possible if there has been fraud, negligent conduct or inadequate disclosure by the taxpayer.

Tax district

2.10   Under the new system each taxpayer will have only one tax district and one tax reference. Having arrived at the quantum of the assessable income by using the Schedular system, all income will be aggregated, less charges and allowances, to arrive at one liability. The taxpayer will file his self-assessment at his tax district and pay the relevant tax accounts office.

Time limits

2.11   Most time limits will be changed to bring them in line with the new filing date of 31 January following the year of assessment. The new general time limit for dealing with tax affairs will become five years from 31 January following the end of the year of assessment, i.e. for 1997/98 the filing date of the tax return will be 31 January 1999 with the normal time limit being to 31 January 2004.

However, most claims will have a specified limit. For those claims required on the tax return the time limit will be one year after the normal filing date for that return, i.e. for 1997/98 the filing date will be 31 January 1999 and the latest date for most claims will be 31 January 2000.

In the case of fraud or negligent conduct the latest date for assessment will be 20 years from 31 January following the tax year, i.e. 31 January 2019 for the tax year 1997/98.

When a taxpayer dies, assessments must be issued within three years of 31 January following the fiscal year of death, i.e. for a death on 6 May 1997 (1997/98), the latest date is 31 January 2002.

Tax returns

2.12   All details shown on a new style tax return will relate to the same fiscal year. This contrasts to the present tax return where income is shown for the current year and allowances for the following year.

As currently, tax returns will not be issued automatically to all taxpayers. A return will be issued to any taxpayer who is known to require a return, i.e. anyone who is self-employed, has a higher rate liability or who is likely to be a special case, e.g. directors, pensioners and those entitled to a tax repayment. It is currently estimated that nine million tax returns will be issued together with a significant number of tax repayment returns.

The current drafts being used by the Inland Revenue indicate that the new tax return will consist of a summary form together with schedules for certain sources of income, allowances or adjustment. The taxpayer will only be required to submit such schedules as are necessary for his individual circumstances. In addition subschedules known as 'help sheets' will be provided on request. Where it is known that a taxpayer will require a help sheet this will be provided automatically.

It is currently anticipated that the tax return will be backed by eight schedules for income and gains, three other schedules and a tax return guide. Although it is unlikely that any taxpayer will have to complete all the schedules, a separate schedule will be required for each separate employment or self-employment. It is therefore quite possible for a taxpayer to have to submit a significant number of schedules.

Filing dates

2.13   Where a return is issued in the normal way, the taxpayer will be required to file the tax return by 31 January following the end of the tax year. There will be an automatic penalty for failure to meet that deadline.

Where a return is issued after 31 October then the normal filing date will be three months from the date on which the return is issued.

If a taxpayer does not wish to work out his own tax liability then the return must be filed by 30 September. If the return is issued after 31 July then the return must be filed within two months of the date of issue if the Inland Revenue is to compute the tax liability.

If a taxpayer submits a tax return without self-assessment after the date mentioned above, i.e. 30 September or two months after the date of issue, then the Revenue will attempt to assess the taxpayer by the due date for payment. If it fails to issue an assessment by that time, then interest will run from the normal due date of payment, not withstanding that the taxpayer will not know his liability at that time because the Revenue has been unable to quantify the liability speedily.

Where a taxpayer submits his tax return after 30 September and is employed then the Revenue will reserve the right to issue a self-assessment showing tax due rather than coding in any underpayment in subsequent years.

Notification of sources of income

2.14 To ensure that the Revenue issues tax returns to all relevant taxpayers the period of time for notification of new sources of income and gains is reduced to six months from the end of the relevant year of assessment, i.e. for income sources arising in 1996/97 notification will be due by 6 October 1997.

The above requirement is not applied where there are no chargeable gains and income is subject to PAYE or to deduction of tax at source to meet the liability. There is, however, a liability to notify the Revenue by 5 October following the end of the year if a higher rate liability arises due to the receipt of investment income taxed at source. A liability to notify also arises if untaxed interest is received.

The new notification period applies for the first time in the tax year 1995/96 requiring notification of new sources of income by 5 October 1996.

If the taxpayer fails to notify the Revenue by 5 October following the end of the fiscal year then he will be liable to a penalty not exceeding the net tax unpaid by 31 January following the year of assessment.

Jean sold quoted shares on 1 June 1996 giving rise to a chargeable gain after annual exemption of £16,800. She did not give notification of chargeability for the year 1996/97 by 5 October 1997. Notice was eventually given to the Revenue of liability on 12 December 1997. £2,000 on account of the tax liability was paid on 30 January 1998.

Her eventual tax liability for the year amounted to £4,200. Jean will be liable to a penalty of an amount not exceeding £2,200.

It should be noted that it is possible that notification of a source of income will be required before the information is available to quantify the income, e.g. John commenced trading on 1 January 1997 making up his accounts to 31 December 1997. The self-employed income source will therefore commence in the tax year 1996/97 and notification will be required by 5 October 1997. By the time that accounts have been prepared for the year to 31 December 1997 the notification date and in practice the date for payment, in the above example 31 January 1998, will have passed. It is therefore essential that all sources of income are notified to the Revenue as soon as they arise. A taxpayer should not wait until such source income can be quantified.

Records

2.15 For the first time a requirement for all taxpayers to keep records for income tax will be introduced in the legislation. This will apply from 1996/97 onwards.

All taxpayers including employed persons will be required to retain all records that have been used to complete their tax return. Such records must be kept until one year after the normal filing date, or, if the return is filed late or amended after the normal filing date one year after the quarter date following the lodgement or amendment date. For this purpose the quarter dates are 31 January, 30 April, 31 July and 31 October.

Example

Joyce files her tax return for 1996/97 on 3 January 1998. The normal filing date is 31 January 1998, therefore her tax records must be maintained until 31 January 1999.

Example

Jason files his tax return for 1996/97 on 2 May 1998. The normal filing date was 31 January 1998, therefore records must be maintained until one year after the quarter date following the date of filing, i.e. date of filing is 2 May 1998, next quarter date is 31 July 1998, records need to be maintained until 31 July 1999.

It should be noted that the above dates correspond to the last day that the Revenue can commence enquiries into a tax return. If the Revenue opens an enquiry, then the records must be maintained until the enquiry is completed.

In the case of a person carrying on a trade, profession or business or who lets property, all tax records must be maintained for five years from 31 January following the year of assessment.

Example

Jennifer lets her holiday home. She files her tax return on 12 December 1997 for the year 1996/97. She must maintain all of her tax records (not just those records that relate to the property letting) until five years after 31 January 1998, i.e. until 31 January 2003.

In the case of a self-employed person or where letting income is involved then the records to be maintained must include details of all amounts received and expended in the course of the trade or business including evidence relating to all receipts and expenditure, e.g. all sales and purchase and expense invoices. The records maintained must include supporting documents, i.e. accounts, books, deeds, contract vouchers, receipts, etc. The documents need not be maintained in their original form but must be in a form that is admissible as evidence. In addition to trading and business records such a taxpayer must also retain dividend vouchers, details of interest received, bank statements and other tax documents for the same period. Failure to comply with this section will give rise to a penalty not exceeding £3,000.

Enquiries into tax returns

2.16   The new tax system brings with it new powers for the Inland Revenue. In future the Revenue will have the statutory power to enquire into any tax return. An officer will not have to give a reason for commencement of an enquiry. However, procedures will have to be followed to open an enquiry and also to formally close an enquiry.

A tax enquiry can be made into the return of an individual, a trustee, a partnership or a company.

The enquiry must be distinguished from the right of the Revenue, and the taxpayer, to correct a tax return. The correction to a tax return, known as a repair, will occur when the Revenue discovers any obvious error or mistake in the return. This can include an error of principle, arithmetical mistakes or any other obvious error. A taxpayer has the right to amend his or her return for any reason. This will include the correction of figures where best estimates have been needed. It will also include the correction of innocent errors, e.g. where interest on a bank account has been overlooked.

When a taxpayer is late filing his tax return then the Revenue's time limit for correction of a return remains at nine months from the date of filing, whereas the individual's time limit for repairing the return remains at one year after 31 January following the end of the year of assessment.

Example

Jonathon files his 1996/97 tax return on 1 June 1998. The due filing date for the return was 31 January 1998. The Revenue may repair the return for a period of nine months, e.g. until 1 March 1999 whereas Jonathon can only repair the return up to 31 January 1999, i.e. twelve months after the normal filing date.

Notification of an enquiry

2.17　If the Revenue decides to enquire into a return, or into an amendment to the return, then it must give written notice to the taxpayer of its intention. If the return was made by the filing date then the Revenue has twelve months from that date to give notification. If the return was filed late then the Revenue has twelve months from the quarter date after the date of filing to give notice. The quarter dates are 31 January, 30 April, 31 July and 31 October.

Example

Jonathon above filed his tax return on 1 June 1998. The following quarter date is 31 July 1998. The Revenue has until 31 July 1999 to issue a notice of enquiry.

Where the taxpayer amends his tax return after the normal filing date, the Revenue has power of enquiry into that amendment as though the return had been filed on the date of amendment.

Example

Jonathon above, who filed his tax return on 1 June 1998 for 1996/97, amends that return on 12 December 1998. The quarter date following the date of amendment is 31 January 1999 and the Revenue can therefore issue a notice of enquiry in respect of the amendment at any time up to 31 January 2000.

Once the Revenue has issued a notice of intention to enquire into a tax return then no amendment of the self-assessment will be possible until the officer has completed his enquiries into the tax return.

Powers to call for documents

2.18   When the Revenue has given notice of its intention to enquire into a tax return, the officer conducting the enquiry may at the same time, or at any subsequent time, require the taxpayer to produce such documents as are needed by the Revenue. Such a notice must be in writing and must specify a time of not less than 30 days by which the taxpayer must produce the documents. It will be noted from the above that the taxpayer is required to keep all such documents that are used to complete his tax return for the period of the potential enquiry. The taxpayer may produce photocopies or facsimile copies of documents, unless the notice specifies that the original documents must be produced. The Revenue can take copies of documents provided to it.

The taxpayer may appeal within 30 days against the notice requiring production of documents. The Commissioners may confirm the notice if it is reasonable, or set it aside. Where there is an appeal, the time limit for the production of the documents is 30 days from the determination by the Commissioners.

Amendments whilst enquiries continue

2.19   During the course of the Revenue's enquiries into a taxpayer's return, the Revenue may come to the conclusion that the tax shown in the self-assessment is too low. Therefore during the course of the enquiry the Revenue may give a notice to the taxpayer to amend his return, and require payment of that additional tax.

Conclusion of enquiry

2.20   On the completion of an enquiry the Revenue again may come to the conclusion that the tax shown in a self-assessment is too low. If an officer of the Revenue forms that opinion then the officer will issue a notice telling the taxpayer what, in the opinion of the Revenue, the self-assessment should have shown. The taxpayer is then given 30 days to amend his self-assessment, informing the Revenue of the same. This enables the taxpayer to amend the tax liability upwards or downwards in line with the officer's conclusions or to make other amendments that the taxpayer considers appropriate.

If the taxpayer does not amend his self-assessment in line with the request of the Inland Revenue within 30 days then the Revenue has a further 30 days in which to correct the return to make good any shortfall the Revenue believes exists. The taxpayer can appeal against any such Revenue amendment.

If the taxpayer believes that the Revenue has no further grounds for enquiry and should complete the enquiries then he can apply to the Commissioners to ask them to direct the Revenue to issue a notice of completion. The Commissioners must give such a direction to the Revenue unless they are satisfied that they have reasonable grounds for proceeding with the enquiry. Such a hearing will be conducted in the same way as an appeal, with both sides being heard and presenting evidence. If the Commissioners decide to issue a notice to the Revenue to direct it to complete the enquiry then the notice given by the Revenue must include the Revenue's conclusions.

Where an enquiry involves a partnership an enquiry into a partnership will also be an enquiry into the tax affairs of each individual taxpayer. However, where a partner is the subject of a tax enquiry into his individual affairs then the Revenue will not necessarily conduct an enquiry into the tax affairs of the other partners. Where there is the completion of a tax enquiry into a partnership then each individual partner will be required to amend his personal tax return within the 30-day time period.

Payment of tax

2.21 The new provisions simplify the payment dates for income tax and capital gains tax. In future, capital gains tax will be due on 31 January following the year of assessment. Income tax will be due on 31 January following the year of assessment, but in most cases the payments on account together with deductions at source will account for the majority of the tax liability. Accordingly only the balance of tax due payable or repayable will be required on 31 January following the end of the year of assessment.

Payments on account

2.22 The payments on account will be based upon the income tax liability of the previous year. This will be the assessable amount of the previous year net of payments of tax at source, e.g. PAYE, SC60 tax, tax credits. One-half of the computed liability for the previous year will be due on 31 January in the fiscal year of assessment. A further payment of the same amount will be due on 31 July following the end of the year of assessment. A further payment of the same amount will be due on 31 July following the end of the year of assessment.

Small payments on account will not be required. The Revenue will be given powers to make regulations setting out de minimis limits. These have not yet been announced. The limits may be absolute, or as a proportion of total income. An indication of the possible limits is given by the tax return draft guide notes which indicate that payments on account will not be required in the following circumstances:

(*a*)   if the tax deducted at source is more than 90% of the total income tax plus Class 4 NIC due; or

(*b*)   if the total tax due is less than £500.

These figures are the tax due for the preceding year used to form the basis of the payments on account for the current year.

Special rules apply to the calculation of interim payments for the transitional year 1996/97 (see Chapter 6). Otherwise the new rules apply from that year.

Example

2.23   Georgina submits her tax return for 1996/97 on 30 January 1998. Her taxation liability for that year is:

	£	£
Income tax		9,250
Capital gains tax		3,000
Class 4 NIC		1,200
		13,450
Less deducted at source	1,800	
paid on account	6,400	8,200
Due 31 January 1998		5,250

With her return, she submits a cheque for the above liability together with payments on accounts for 1997/98 calculated in the following way (based upon 1996/97 return figures):

Income tax	9,250
Class 4 NIC	1,200
	10,450
Less deducted at source	1,800
Relevant amount	8,650

(*Note:* the liability is NOT recalculated using 1997/98 rates or allowances.)

```
Due 31 January 1998 50% x 8,650      £4,325
       31 July 1998 50% x £8,650      £4,325
```

Her tax return for 1997/98, submitted on 30 November 1998, shows taxation liabilities of:

		£
Income tax		10,400
Capital gains tax		Nil
Class 4 NIC		1,250
		11,650
Less deducted at source	1,750	
payments on account	8,650	10,400
Due 31 January 1999		1,250

Her payment will also include a payment on account for 1998/99 of:

	£
Income tax and Class 4 (as above)	11,650
Less deducted at source	1,750
	9,900

50% thereof = £4,950

If the payments on account exceed the liability then repayment will be made by the Revenue on 31 January following the year of assessment. If repayment is not made by 31 January, interest will be added from that date.

Reduction of payments on account

2.24   Where a taxpayer believes that the amount due for the current tax year will be less than in the previous year, an application may be made at any time before 31 January following the year of assessment for the payments on account to be reduced. The payments on account may be reduced to nil by a *Taxes Management Act 1970, s 59A* claim, or reduced to a specified amount by a similar claim. The claim must set out the reason for the application to reduce the payments on account. If appropriate, repayment of tax already paid will be made to the taxpayer at that time. However, if a taxpayer fraudulently or negligently makes an incorrect statement in connection with such a claim he will be liable to a penalty not exceeding the excess of the correct tax over the actual tax paid on account.

It is understood that, in practice, the Revenue will accept all reasonable claims under this section without query.

Example

2.25   Georgina retires on 1 December 1998. She estimates that she will have no liability to income tax or Class 4 NIC for 1998/99. She makes a claim on 1 March 1990 indicating that no payments on account are due.

The Revenue will repay the £4,950 paid on 31 January 1999 and no amount will be due on 31 July 1999.

Her tax return for 1998/99, submitted on 20 December 1999, shows taxation liabilities of:

	£
Income tax	4,100
Capital gains	1,800
Class 4 NIC	700
	6,600
Less deducted at source	1,400
Payable 31 January 2000	5,200

If the Revenue believed that her claim had been made fraudulently or negligently then the maximum penalty would be

	£
Income tax	4,100
Class 4 NIC	700
	4,800
Less deducted at source	1,400
Maximum penalty	3,400

The taxpayer can make a claim to reduce payments on account by a stated amount. In those circumstances the maximum penalty for negligent claims would be reduced further by the amounts paid on account. It is expected that the Revenue will only take penalties where the amounts involved are material.

Information required to compute tax payment

2.26   When computing tax payments, it must be remembered that it will not be possible to use such statements as 'as returned' in a tax return. To complete a return for an employed person it will be necessary to have sight of forms P60 and P11D or P9D. It will also be necessary to have all coding notices relating to the year in order to be able to compute the income tax paid that relates to the current year. Where more than one employment has been involved such documents will be required for all employments. If appropriate part 1A of form P45 will be required to detail the income and tax paid in respect of earlier employments. The self-assessment rules apply to the collection of underpaid Schedule E except where the return is filed by 30 September following the end of the tax year when the Revenue will code in underpayments of under £1,000.

To compute the tax payment the taxpayer can calculate the liability due in his own way, or use the working sheets provided in the tax guide. These are discussed in detail in Chapter 10. Essentially the sheets summarise income, deductions, allowances and other information required to compute the liability to tax, e.g. dividends. From the computed tax in working sheet 5 the tax paid for the year by way of deduction at source and tax credits can be deducted. This is summarised in working sheet 4.

Where tax underpaid for an earlier year has been included in the PAYE of the current year it is necessary to deduct that tax underpayment of the earlier year from the tax paid in the year. This is done in working sheet 5. Furthermore where the Revenue is aware of an underpayment arising from employment during the year and has notified that it will incorporate that underpayment in PAYE code for a later year then the notified amount must be deducted from the liability of the year to arrive at the amount of liability payable for the year. Again this is done in working sheet 5.

Amendments and repairs

2.27   Where a taxpayer amends his self-assessment, including circumstances where the Revenue has repaired the tax return, i.e. given notice to the taxpayer to amend his self-assessment, then the revised tax is payable on the normal due date or 30 days after the making of the revised self-assessment. Interest is charged from the normal due date if earlier. It should be noted that the amendment to a tax return will affect the amount of payments on account required for the following year as well as amending the tax due for the year of change.

Notification that payment is due

2.28   Where the Revenue is aware of a tax liability before the due date it is their intention to notify the taxpayer of the need to make a remittance, i.e. if the 1996/97 tax return had been submitted with the self-assessment duly completed by 31 October 1997 then it is anticipated that the Revenue would issue a notice of tax due as at 31 January 1998 during January 1998. In the same way the Revenue would issue a reminder for the payment due on 31 July 1998. The Revenue has no statutory obligation to issue such reminders. The taxpayer's liabilities and payments will all be dealt with by one office. Accordingly every time the Revenue issues details it will produce a 'credit card style' statement showing liabilities, payments made, penalties, surcharges and interest to date. It is anticipated that such a statement will be issued every time there is a movement on the account.

Chapter 3

Self-Assessment — what it will mean for Employers

3.1 The introduction of the self-assessment tax returns will mean that employers will have to provide detailed information to employees relating to amounts earned from employment in cash and kind at an early stage. Failure to provide such information timeously would mean that the employee could not complete his personal tax return and as such would be liable to a penalty.

The Inland Revenue has conducted extensive consultation to ensure that sufficient information is provided to employees in time for them to complete their personal tax returns whilst at the same time minimising the impact upon employers.

3.2 It must be remembered that the term employer includes anyone who pays a wage, fee, salary or other benefits to someone working for them under a contract of service, and also includes anyone who pays a pension to a pensioner.

Provision of information to employees

P60 — year end summary of pay and deductions

3.3 The employer is currently required to deduct PAYE and National Insurance at source before making payments to an employee, etc. A summary of gross pay and tax (and NI) deducted at source is prepared at the end of each year. This is in three parts, the top two parts known as P14 are sent to the Inland Revenue (with one copy forwarded by them to DSS) and the third copy known as form P60 is given to an employee. Currently there is no time limit for giving form P60 (certificate of pay and tax deductions) to the employee. From 6 April 1997 the P60 will have to be given to the employee by 31 May after the end of the tax year, i.e. for 1996/97 the deadline is 31 May 1997.

3.4 The employer is free to provide the P60 in the way that is most convenient. This could be by post, by hand with payslips, etc.

Although many small employers will provide the information on the three-part Revenue form others will produce the information on an agreed computerised system.

3.5   Employers are required to give form P60 to employees who are working for them at 5 April. Failure to provide a copy to the employee will give rise to the same penalty as failure to supply forms P14 or equivalent to the Inland Revenue by 19 May following the end of the fiscal year. The initial penalty is up to £300 per form. If an employer does not provide information then it can be required to do so by the General or Special Commissioners against a further penalty of up to £60 per form per day that failure continues.

Former employees

3.6   An employer is also required to prepare a form P14 for anyone who had worked with it during the fiscal year, or for whom deductions were required (e.g. Class 1A National Insurance charge on a car provided in the previous fiscal year). An employer may continue to give a copy of that form to past employees if it so wishes but is not under a statutory obligation to do so.

P45 — details of employee leaving

3.7   Instead, when an employee leaves, a revised form P45 must be used. This new, four-part form must be used for all employees who leave after 6 April 1996. In addition to the existing information the form will have a further insert known as part 1A. This will show the gross pay and tax deducted by the employer during the period of employment in the current fiscal year. The information on P45 part 1A will need to be used by the employee to complete his personal tax return. Accordingly employees must keep such forms safely.

As at present part 1 of the form P45 must be sent by the old employer to the tax office. Parts 1A, 2 and 3 are handed to the employee. The employee must detach and keep part 1A and give parts 2 and 3 to the new employer. The new employer must complete part 3 forwarding the same to its PAYE district and retaining part 2 for its own records.

The information provided on form P45 will be similar to that currently provided, but in addition the form will show details of pay and tax from the current employment as well as the cumulative pay and tax to date. This additional information will not be required to be completed where it is the same as the cumulative pay and tax.

3.8   Where an employee moves jobs within a group of companies it is often agreed that form P45 is not given to the employee but dealt with by the employer. From 6 April 1996 employers moving employees within their organisation will be required to provide the relevant employees with pay and tax details in respect of each job. Therefore, although they need not give them a form P45 they must provide the information shown on form 1A at the time that the employee changes his position within the organisation. This is so that the employee can show on his tax return the amount of pay received and tax deducted in respect of each separate employment.

P9D/P11D — return of benefits in kind

3.9   In addition to providing details of pay and tax deducted an employer is required to make a return of expense payments and benefits. In the case of employees earning at a rate of £8,500 per annum or more the form is P11D. In the case of other employees it is form P9D.

3.10   In determining which form to use an employer must look at the rate at which an employee is earning rather than the amount earned in a fiscal year. To the actual pay must be added all expense payments and benefits before deducting allowable expenses other than ordinary annual contributions to an approved superannuation fund including additional voluntary contributions (AVCs) and payroll giving. The benefits and expenses include:

(a)   the higher of the car benefit and car fuel benefit charges and the cash alternative of a salary sacrifice;

(b)   the amounts chargeable under all of the other benefits sections including reimbursed car expenses, vouchers or credit cards provided by the employer; and

(c)   the settling by the employer of a debt incurred personally by the individual in respect of motoring expenses. [*FA 1995, s 43* amending *ICTA 1988, s 167*]. Form P11D is also required for each director whatever his or her rate of remuneration except those earning at a rate of less than £8,500 per annum who are full-time working directors without a material interest in the company, or a director of a non-profit-making concern or charity.

Where an employee holds a number of employments with connected companies all remuneration must be aggregated for the purpose of deciding whether the individual is paid at a rate of £8,500 per annum or more.

3.11   For those employees not caught by the P11D legislation form P9D is used. This is a return of expense payments and income from tax cannot be deducted. It requires a return of the amount of expenses not included in the pay records, amounts paid in respect of vouchers, credit cards, accommodation and gifts in kind. Further it provides details of pecuniary liabilities of employees met by the employer including personal telephone bills, National Insurance, etc. A reference number by each entry refers to the space on the tax return to be used by the employee in reporting the same information to the Inland Revenue.

3.12   From 1996/97 the deadline for sending forms P9D or P11D to the Inland Revenue becomes 6 July. The penalty for failure to file will be an initial penalty of up to £300 per form imposed by the General or Special Commissioners. Failure to file can then result in a further penalty of up to £60 per form per day that the failure continues. Under the new legislation a copy of forms P9D or P11D is to be given to the employee. Failure to provide the form to the employee by the same deadline of 6 July can give rise to similar penalties.

3.13   An employer will be required to give a copy of forms P9D/ P11D to each employee in his employment on 5 April. This can be provided to the employee in the way most convenient to the employer. For employees who have left employment between 5 April and the date of providing the form the employer can satisfy the legislation by posting the form to the last known address of the employee.

3.14   An employer will not automatically have to give a copy of forms P9D/P11D to employees who have left during the tax year. However, such employees will require the information shown upon the form if they receive a tax return for completion. Accordingly it is provided that such an ex-employee may request a copy of the form from his previous employer. The employee must make a written request to the employer within 3 years of the end of the tax year. The employer must provide the information within 30 days of the written request, or 6 July following the end of the relevant tax year if later. He can make only one request. An employer is then obliged to provide the information shown on forms P9D/P11D.

In practice employers may find that it is more convenient to provide copies of forms P9D/P11D automatically to all employees and ex-employees at the same time.

3.15   The format of the provision of the information to employees will be at the discretion of the employer. Small employers may prefer to photocopy the Revenue form, whereas those providing information on computer spreadsheets to the Revenue will need to set up a system which provides individual output for each of the employees. There will be no set format although it would be helpful if such spreadsheets provided the information in the same order as that shown on the individual's tax return. The official forms P9D/P11D will have a reference by each box indicating the equivalent reference on the tax return where the amount should be entered. Employers producing computer spreadsheet information should include the same references, and to assist the completion of the employee's tax return, the information should be provided in the same order as that used on the tax return.

3.16 The new forms P9D/P11D will require the provision of similar information to that currently provided, that is, details of the gross cost of benefits and expenses to the employer including VAT. The form will show a deduction of amounts made good by the employee, or amounts on which tax has been paid to arrive at the cash equivalent. The employee will still be required to make his or her own 'Section 198' claim for expenses on his personal tax return. This will include a claim for reimbursed expenses incurred wholly, exclusively and necessarily in the performance of the duties of the employment. This requirement together with the reporting requirement on form P9D/P11D will be avoided where the employer has a dispensation in force (see 3.26 below). To enable an employee to determine whether a deduction is possible in respect of entertaining costs borne by the employer, the employer will be required to indicate on form P11D whether the business is a trade, profession or vocation and that the amounts shown as entertaining have been disallowed in the employer's tax computations. A tick will indicate that the employee may make an expenses claim against the item whereas a cross will indicate that no such claim will be possible.

Third party benefits

3.17 In addition to reporting expenses and benefits provided by the employer to the employee there will be reporting requirements from 6 April 1996 in respect of benefits provided by a third party to the employees of an employer where the employer has arranged for that other person to provide the benefit. The term arranged will include the guaranteeing of the provision of benefits by a third party or the facilitation of the provision by a third party. In all cases the employer will have to be actively involved in the provision of benefits to be required to report the same on form P11D.

3.18 An employer would be regarded as having arranged benefits or expenses to its employees where another group company has provided the benefit or expense payment. In the same way where one employer agrees with another non-connected employer to provide reciprocal benefits or expenses including the provision of goods or services to each other's employees free or at a discount, then each employer would be regarded as having arranged the provision to its own employees.

Where an employer is deemed to have arranged a benefit then the employer will be responsible for reporting the cash equivalent on form P11D.

3.19 An employer would not be deemed to have arranged a benefit where it has not been actively involved in the provision of that expense payment or benefit. The mere contact between an employer and a third party would not be arrangements for this purpose. Therefore, if the employer had merely provided a list of employees to a third party there would be no reporting requirement. In the same way where a business as a matter of custom or practice of the particular industry provides free or cheap goods or services to employees of another employer without the involvement of the employer again there would be no reporting requirement on the main employer.

3.20 Where employers agree with retailers for the retailer to offer a small discount on goods to their employees there may be an arrangement, however, no amount would have to be declared on form P11D as long as the retailer was charging an amount which was not less than cost of the items concerned. Using the principle established in the case of *Pepper v Hart* the declarable amount is the marginal additional cost and in this instance there would be no marginal additional cost and therefore no declarable amount even though the arrangements in principle gave the employer the duty to declare such benefits on the employee's form P11D.

As will be seen the only time that there is a reporting requirement on the employer is where it has had an active involvement with the third party. In those circumstances full details of the costs involved of providing the expenses or benefits should be readily available to the employer. If, however, such information is not available, e.g. the third party refuses to disclose the costs involved, the employer must complete form P11D with a best estimate marking the amount accordingly.

3.21 Where an employer has not actively facilitated a third party benefit then the responsibility for the provision of information passes to the third party.

From 1996/97 onwards where a third party makes an expense payment, or provides benefits in kind to employees of another employer then the third party will have to provide to the recipients the same details as would be required from the employer. That is to say that the third party must in writing provide the recipient with the cash equivalent of any benefit in kind. The information must be given to the recipient by 6 July following the end of the tax year.

Although third parties have to provide the information to employees they do not have to provide the information directly to the Inland Revenue unless the Revenue has issued a return under *section 15* of the *Taxes Management Act 1970.*

3.22 There will be no set format in which the third party provides information. It can choose a method that is most convenient to itself. Accordingly it will be possible to provide details of the payments each time a payment is made or benefit provided or alternatively will be able to make a yearly return to the recipient. The information may be provided by hand, by post or via the employer.

Although third parties are required to provide details of the cash equivalent of benefits and expenses there will be no reporting requirements in respect of goodwill, entertainment or small gifts costing (in total) £100 or less to the provider. These provisions only apply if the provider is not the employer nor a person connected with the employer and the employer has not directly or indirectly procured the provision of the benefit. The benefit must not be made either in recognition of the performance of particular services in the course of employment or in anticipation of services which are to be performed. The third party will not have to report tips or items included within a taxed awards scheme, although these items are still taxable receipts in the hands of the employee.

Taxed awards

3.23 Where an employer or a third party provides a benefit under the taxed awards scheme the provider meets the tax liability on the non-cash incentive prices. The provider then gives the recipient a certificate showing the amounts to be included on the individual's tax return.

Motor vehicles

3.24 Where an employer provides a motor vehicle for an employee it will be required to compute the car benefit charge arising and if appropriate the car fuel benefit charge. It is anticipated that working sheets will be provided to supplement the P11D in respect of cars. As for National Insurance the employer will be required to state the business mileage undertaken in each car. If mileage records are not available then the employer must base the cash equivalent on the assumption that fewer than 2,500 business miles per annum had been travelled by the employee.

If an employee uses his own motor vehicle for business then details must be provided of the car or mileage allowance paid in respect of the employee's car. This includes payments made using the rates published by the Inland Revenue for the fixed profit car scheme. To avoid the need to make a return of mileage payments the employer must either formally join the fixed profit car scheme or obtain a dispensation from the Revenue to make such payments.

Fixed profit car schemes (FPCS)

3.25 Where an employer has joined the fixed profit car scheme it will complete form FPCS2 showing the gross amount paid to the employee and the business miles travelled. The employer will then compute the profit element of the payment over the scale allowances. This amount must be included by the employee upon his personal tax return. To enable the employee to have the information a copy of form FPCS2 must be given to the employee by 6 July following the end of the tax year.

Dispensations

3.26 Dispensations are available to reduce the reporting requirements of employers and employees. Where an employer formally asks the Inland Revenue for a dispensation and it is granted then the employer does not have to include details of such expenses on forms P11D, P9D or supplementary forms. The employee is not required to declare the expenses received on his personal tax return and is not required to make an expenses claim under *ICTA 1988, s 198.*

The Inland Revenue will consider a dispensation for expense payments or benefits in kind where no tax will be payable by the employee because he/she can claim a matching tax deduction. Dispensations will be given for payments of travelling and subsistence on an approved scale for business journeys. It may be possible to get dispensations for other expenses incurred. These could include reimbursed expenditure, professional subscriptions and business telephone calls. It is not the practice of the Revenue to grant dispensations for entertainment expenses, for expenditure abroad or where the person making the claim is also the individual responsible for checking the claim. Dispensations will not be granted for round sum allowances.

3.27 The Inland Revenue is currently encouraging employers to make dispensation applications in respect of normal expenses and benefits not giving rise to a taxable amount. Employers should seriously consider making application for dispensations for travelling and subsistence, etc. before the introduction of the revised rules, i.e. before 6 April 1996. This should minimise the information to be provided on forms P11D and also reduce the number of forms to be completed. Application is made to the Inspector dealing with PAYE. More details can be obtained from any tax office, or in leaflet IR69 'Expenses: form P11D'.

Where a dispensation is obtained it must be noted that any change will invalidate the dispensation. Care should therefore be taken to obtain the dispensation in general terms, e.g. mileage allowances paid in accordance with the current FPCS rates.

Annual voluntary settlements

3.28 Where an annual voluntary settlement (AVS) is in force, that is an arrangement between an employer and the Inland Revenue by which the employer pays tax and National Insurance contributions due on certain expense payments or benefits then no further entries will be required on form P11D. It should be noted that under the AVS arrangements the tax is computed by grossing up the benefits. Although there is no requirement for employers to tell the employees details of voluntary settlements, or dispensations, it is likely to be in the best interests of the employer to provide the employees with information. This should reduce the number of queries from employees in respect of benefit payments. Information could be provided to employees at the time that employment commences, when dispensations or AVSs are agreed with the Revenue, with form P11D each year or via company magazines or information sheets. As AVSs are usually agreed after the end of the year it may be that it is best to tell employees about such settlements with form P11D.

Filing dates

3.29 Forms P9D/P11D and associated documents have to be filed with the Inland Revenue by 6 July following the end of the tax year, e.g. for 1996/97 by 6 July 1997. Under the new provisions a copy of such information must be provided to the employee by the same date. Information must be provided to ex-employees on request and provided to recipients of benefits by third parties again by 6 July.

Penalties

3.30 Where the information provided is incorrect or incomplete the legislation provides for a maximum penalty of £3,000 for each incorrect or incomplete form. [*TMA 1970, s 98(2)*]. However, the Revenue will normally usually invite the employer to give an explanation as to why the form is incorrect before any penalty action is taken. If the error or omission is entirely innocent no penalty will arise. The maximum penalty would only be imposed in the most exceptional of circumstances.

The information has to be provided to the employees. Failure to file the forms with the Inland Revenue or to provide information to the employees would give rise to an initial penalty imposed by the General or Special Commissioners of up to £300 per form plus a further penalty of up to £60 per form for each day that failure continues. [*TMA 1970, s 98(1)*]. It is likely that the Revenue will only pursue penalties where the amounts of tax involved are significant or the employer persists in failing to comply. However, as failure to give the information to the employee could result in the employee not being able to complete his own tax return, and thereby suffering a penalty in his own name, the Revenue will take action where an employee tells it of an employer's failure to comply with its obligations.

Similar rules apply in respect of form P60 where the time limit for provision to the employee is 31 May.

Chapter 4

Self-Assessment — what it will mean for Employees

Introduction

4.1   The first consultative document heralding the introduction of the new system of self-assessment was entitled 'A simpler system for the taxing of the self-employed'. This document proposed significant changes for the self-employed and hinted at wider changes. These only became apparent in November 1992 when a second consultative document was published entitled 'A simpler system for assessing personal tax'. The intention to alter the whole tax assessment system then became clear.

In March 1993 the Chancellor announced that from 1996/97 all taxpayers would be subject to the self-assessment regime. This means that the onerous task of being responsible for assessments is moved from the Inland Revenue to the taxpayer. However, it does not mean that taxpayers, including employees, have to self-assess. Instead if they complete their tax return and submit the same to the Inland Revenue by 30 September (or two months after the issue of the return if later) following the end of the fiscal year then the Inland Revenue will quantify the amount of the tax due. The resultant calculation is known as a self-assessment and the employee is still responsible for its contents.

The operation of the PAYE system for employees has meant that many employed persons have not received tax returns. Traditionally the Revenue issues a return on demand or issues tax returns to employees who are known to have other income, claims for allowances, a liability to higher rate tax or directorships. In addition the Revenue issues returns on cessation of work where appropriate. This means as many as 21 million UK taxpayers do not receive a tax return each year.

Self-assessment and employees

4.2   The new system will continue to achieve the economies of the previous system and returns will not be issued automatically to each taxpayer. However, when an employee needs a tax return, or is issued with a tax return then the self-assessment regime will apply.

4.3 *Self-Assessment — what it will mean for Employees*

If a return is issued and not filed by the due date then a penalty will apply.

The method of collecting tax under PAYE will continue as before. This means that even those employees receiving tax returns will not necessarily have to make payments directly to the Revenue. The new regime will provide that if the calculated tax underpaid for a year is less than £1,000 then it will automatically be collected by way of code number adjustments in subsequent years. This will only apply provided the return is filed with the Revenue by 30 September. Alternatively an employee may pay the underpayment directly to the Revenue by ticking the appropriate box on the tax return. Payment may be compulsory where the return is filed after 30 September following the end of the fiscal year.

Although it is not anticipated that the Revenue will widely use its powers, the new regime will allow the Revenue to conduct investigations into the affairs of employees. The majority of such investigations will take place where the Revenue believes that there have been errors in the tax affairs of the taxpayer. However, for statistical reasons a sample of employees will be selected each year for tax audit.

4.3   Unlike the self-employed, employees are already taxed on an actual basis. This will continue under self-assessment. The basis of assessment of an employee is the income paid or deemed paid in a fiscal year. Income is deemed to be paid if it is made available to the employee whether or not the employee actually draws the emolument. In the case of directors there are further tests that also apply. The date of payment is the earlier of:

(*a*)   date of payment;

(*b*)   entitlement to payment;

(*c*)   date that emoluments are credited in the company accounts;

(*d*)   where emoluments are determined before an accounting period ends the last day of the accounting period; and

(*e*)   where emoluments are determined after the end of an accounting period the date of determination. [*ICTA 1988, s 202B*].

Retention of information

4.4   An employee must provide information to the Inland Revenue of his total earnings and benefits from each separate employment held during a fiscal year. This will require the completion of a separate schedule for each job. In order that the employee can do this he must retain his form P60. The legislation provides that from 1996/97 an employer must provide a copy of P60 to the employee by 31 May following the end of the fiscal year. In addition the employee will require form P11D (or if lower paid form P9D) giving details of benefits and expenses provided by the employer, this will be provided by 6 July. If the employee has had a former employment during the fiscal year then part 1A of form P45 (issued on change of employment) will be required for the earlier employment to show the tax deducted and pay earned at that former employment. If benefits were provided by the former employer then the employee will have to request a copy of form P11D (unless provided automatically). An employee must make such a written request to his former employer within 3 years of the end of the tax year. The employer must provide a copy of the P11D to the ex-employee within 30 days of the written request (or 6 July after the end of the relevant tax year) if later. An employee can only make one request for such a copy of form P11D.

4.5   If an employee receives benefits from a third party then the third party must provide a written notice setting out the taxable benefit received. However, certain amounts will not receive any notification, e.g. tips. These are still required to be included upon the tax return as in earlier years.

Expenses

4.6   An employee will be entitled to make a claim for any expenditure incurred wholly, exclusively and necessarily in the performance of the duties of the employment. This claim must be made on Schedule 1 of the tax return.

4.7   Where an employer has a dispensation for expense payments then the amounts will not have to be included as income and an expense claim will not be required by the employee. It is anticipated that employers will provide details of dispensation in force to employees so that they will be aware of the existence of the dispensation and of the fact that no entries will be required in respect of payments thereunder.

An employee will also be able to make a claim for fixed deductions where trade unions or other relevant bodies have agreed with the Inland Revenue a fixed deduction in respect of expenses. Taxpayers who are members of professional bodies may claim a deduction for the annual subscription to such bodies provided that the subscription is required for the duties of the employment and the professional body has obtained the agreement of the Revenue to a deduction.

4.8 Although most employees will not complete tax returns, there will be a statutory obligation upon all taxpayers including employees to maintain such records that are necessary to complete a tax return. Such records must be maintained for one year from 31 January following the fiscal year of assessment. This is increased to five years if the income includes income from a trade, profession, vocation or from property lettings. The penalty for failure to retain records is an amount of up to £3,000. [*TMA 1970, s 12B(5)*].

Chapter 5

The Penalty Regime

Penalties on employees

Enforcement

5.1   In order to control and police a self-assessment system it is necessary to have a comprehensive armoury of penalties available to the Revenue authority. The proposal for income tax self-assessment is no exception. The Revenue will automatically charge interest from the due date of payment. To compensate, a repayment of interest will be paid on overpaid tax from the due date or payment date, whichever is the later.

In addition to interest for late payment, there will be a surcharge if tax is not paid by 28 days from the final due date. This surcharge increases by a further surcharge of 5% of the tax unpaid 6 months after the normal due date. Such a surcharge is treated as though it is income tax for the purpose of charging interest. However, a surcharge is not taken in addition to a further tax-geared penalty.

For the first time an automatic penalty applies for failure to file an income tax return by the due date. If a return is not filed by 31 January following the end of the fiscal year, or three months after the date of issue if later (providing full notification of liability has been made), then there will be a penalty of £100. If the return has not been filed by six months after the filing date, a further penalty of £100 is imposed. The Commissioners can set aside the flat penalty if there is a reasonable excuse for failure.

If the failure continues after a year, a penalty can be imposed up to the tax liability that would have been shown in the return. On application by the Revenue to the Commissioners, a daily penalty can be imposed.

Similar penalties apply to each partner for failure to file a partnership return.

5.2   The Penalty Regime

The new regime makes it essential that full records relating to income are maintained and tax returns are filed by the due date. In addition tax must be paid by the due date. The penalties for failure to meet such deadlines can be high.

Interest

5.2   Interest is charged on late-paid tax and on any surcharges added to the tax. Interest is also charged on penalties, from the due date to the payment date.

Interest is charged on income and capital gains tax from the due date of payment until the actual date of payment. This applies to payments on account as well as to the final payment on 31 January following the end of the tax year. In the case of a cheque the payment date is the date it is received by the Revenue, providing it is honoured on presentation.

Amendments to tax returns

5.3   If a tax return is amended, interest applies from the normal final payment date. However, it would appear that an amendment to a tax return will also amend the payments on account due for the following year, which in itself will give rise to an additional interest charge from the normal payment date to the actual date of payment.

Interest on payments on account where eventual liability exceeds preceding year liability

5.4   If a taxpayer believes that the payments on account to be made are too high then he may make application to reduce those payments. This is known as a *Taxes Management Act 1970, s 59A* claim. Where a claim has been made to reduce the payments on account to nil, or to reduce the payments on account then special rules apply to calculate the interest payable.

Interest will be charged on the basis that the amount collectable on account is the lower of:

(*a*)   the original payment on account (50% of preceding year liability); or

(*b*)   one-half of the final liability (50% of current year liability).

The interest due will then be calculated on the difference between the actual payment and the deemed payment on account under the above rule.

If the estimate proves too low, then interest may be payable from the normal payment date for the payment on account to the actual date of payment. In most instances the actual date of payment will be the date of the final payment.

In normal circumstances, this means that interest will be charged on the difference between the amount paid and the normal payment account had a claim for reduction not been made. If one-half of the eventual final income tax liability is lower than the payment on account based upon the previous year's liability then interest will be restricted to that lower figure.

Example

5.5   Donna has an income tax liability for 1997/98 of £10,000. Accordingly, £5,000 is payable on 31 January 1999 and 31 July 1999 as payments on account of 1998/99.

She is aware that her income for the current year will be reduced because of falling profits and she makes a claim under *TMA 1970, s 59A(4)* to reduce her payments on account to £3,500 on each occasion, which she pays on time.

Her eventual income tax liability for 1998/99 amounts to £8,200, which she settles with a final payment of £1,200 on 30 January 2000.

Interest will be due on later payments on account as follows:

	£
Original payment on account	5,000
One-half of collectable liability	
50% x £8,200	4,100
Difference between actual payment	3,500
and lower of the above	4,100
	600

Interest is due on:

Period	
1 February 1999 to 31 July 1999	600
1 August 1999 to 30 January 2000	1,200

Example

5.6   Continuing the above example for 1999/2000, Donna has a liability to pay payments on account of £4,100 on 31 January 2000 and on 31 July 2000. She again makes a *TMA 1970, s 59A(4)* claim to reduce her payments on account to £3,900 on each date. However, her eventual liability for the year 1999/2000 amounts to £9,100, which she settles with a final payment on 20 February 2001.

Interest will be due on payments on account as follows:

	£
Original payment on account	4,100
One-half of collectable liability	
50% x £9,100	4,550
Difference between actual payment	3,900
and lower of above	4,100
	200

Thus, although the final payment for 1999/2000 will amount to £9,100 - (£3,900 + £3,900) = £1,300, interest will only be charged on late payments on account of £200 from 31 January 2000 and a further £200 from 31 July 2000 giving interest due on:

	£
Period 1 February 2000 to 31 July 2000	200
1 August 2000 to 31 January 2001	400
1 February 2001 to 20 February 2001	1,300

together with interest on the late paid 2000/2001 payment on account:

1 February 2001 to 20 February 2001   4,550

Interest remitted where eventual liability is lower than payment on account

5.7   Similar calculations are to be made where interest is charged on payments on account made late where there is an eventual repayment of tax.

If interest has been charged on late payments on account and eventually there is no liability whatsoever for the year, then all interest charged on late payments on account will be remitted.

If the payments on account exceed the eventual total liability for the year, and one or both of the payments on account have been paid late, then the payments on account are deemed to have been reduced to one-half of the eventual total liability. Insofar as any interest charged relates to the excess of payments on account over revised liability, it will be remitted.

Example

5.8   Ann has a liability to pay interim tax for 1997/98 of £2,100 on each occasion. She makes the payments on 31 March 1998, and 28 October 1998 with interest being charged on late payment of:

First instalment	£36
Second instalment	£51

Her liability for that year is self-assessed at £2,800 with repayment made to her of £1,400.

Interest will be remitted on one-half of the repayment (£700) restricted to the payment on account due (£2,100) in respect of each payment on account, i.e. she would receive a repayment of £1,400 plus remitted interest on late payment of:

700/2,100 x £36 =		£12
and 700/2,100 x £51 =		£17
		£29

The new rules on interest apply from 1996/97 onwards.

Surcharges

5.9   To prevent the taxpayer using the Inland Revenue as a cheap form of loan finance a surcharge will be payable where the final liability is not paid timeously.

The new surcharge section provides that where tax remains unpaid 28 days from the due date it shall be increased by a surcharge of 5%. Furthermore, when any tax remains unpaid on the day following the expiry of six months from the due date, the surcharge on the tax then outstanding is a further 5%. The surcharge will not be charged as well as a tax-geared penalty.

The surcharge will be charged by way of notice served by the Revenue on the taxpayer. The taxpayer may appeal against that notice within 30 days. The Commissioners may set aside the surcharge if it appears to them that the taxpayer had a reasonable excuse throughout the period of default for not paying the tax. The inability to pay the tax is not in itself a reasonable excuse. Alternatively, the Board of the Inland Revenue may mitigate or remit the surcharge at its discretion.

Interest will be charged on any surcharge not paid within 30 days of the date that the notice is issued. A surcharge is not charged on late-paid payments on account.

Repairs and amendments

5.10 In the same way, if a tax return is repaired by the Revenue or amended by the taxpayer, then the due date for payment becomes 30 days after the notice of amendment.

Similar rules apply where a self-assessment is amended following enquiries by the Revenue. Such enquiries will result in a notice of completion, which must state the Revenue's conclusions as to the amount of tax which should be contained in the taxpayer's self-assessment. The taxpayer then has 30 days in which to amend his return, and a further 30 days after that in which to pay the tax. If the tax remains unpaid 28 days following the end of that latter period, then a surcharge will be applied.

If the taxpayer disagrees with the Revenue, then the Revenue will itself amend the assessment. The taxpayer will have the right to appeal against the amended assessment and to postpone the additional tax at that time.

A worked example of interest and surcharge

5.11 Susan has a final liability for 1996/97, due 31 January 1998, of £2,100. She pays £1,000 on 28 February 1998. On 31 March 1998 the Revenue issues a notice of surcharge. She pays a further £600 on 31 May 1998. On 2 August 1998 the Revenue issues a further surcharge notice. Susan pays the balance of her liability and surcharges on 31 August 1998. Her interest and surcharge payable will be (assuming 10% p.a. interest):

Surcharge

	£	£
On tax outstanding at 28 February 1998		
5% x £1,100	55	
On tax outstanding at 31 July 1998		
5% x £500	25	80

Interest	£	£
1 February to 28 February		
10% x 28/365 x £2,100	16	
1 March to 30 April		
10% x 61/365 x £1,100	18	
1 May to 31 May		
10% x 31/365 x £1,155	10	
(including surcharge unpaid after 30 days)		
1 June to 31 August		
10% x 92/365 x £555	14	58
		138

(Note that the second surcharge is paid within 30 days of the notice and therefore does not attract interest.)

Assessments and determinations

Determination of tax where no return delivered

5.12 Under self-assessment, the Revenue will not normally issue an assessment to the taxpayer. However, if a taxpayer does not file a completed return when a form has been sent to him then the Revenue will be able to raise a determination on him. Such a determination will be treated as if it were a self-assessment. The Revenue will make the determination to the best of its information and belief and it may be based upon income tax or capital gains tax for the year of assessment.

Any tax payable under the determination is deemed to be due on the same day as the normal tax which would have been due had the taxpayer self-assessed. This tax is collectable and cannot be postponed. A self-assessment filed within twelve months of the date of determination will supersede the determination.

The Revenue cannot issue a determination more than five years after 31 January following the year of assessment.

The above provisions deal with the situation where the taxpayer has now filed a tax return. It should be remembered that the onus is on the taxpayer to report sources of income within six months from the end of the fiscal year in which those sources arise. Failure to do so will give rise to the penalties, i.e. an amount not exceeding the amount assessable for the year or the amount not paid by the due date (see also 5.15 below).

Assessment where a loss of tax is discovered

5.13   A less common situation may well be where the taxpayer has not notified the Revenue of a source of income and therefore a tax return has not been submitted. Then the Revenue may raise an assessment when a loss of tax is discovered by it.

If the Revenue is unhappy with the information provided by a tax return then it may enquire into the tax return.

As the enquiry system does not of itself give rise to penalties it must be expected that the Revenue will be looking to make 'discoveries' during the course of an enquiry, thus enabling it to issue assessments and charge penalties.

An assessment may be raised if an officer discovers:

(*a*)   that any profits which ought to have been assessed to tax have not been assessed;

(*b*)   that an assessment to tax is or has become insufficient; or

(*c*)   that any relief which has been given is or has become excessive.

It is not a discovery if the taxpayer has delivered a return and that return was made in accordance with the normally accepted accounting practice prevailing at the time when the return was made.

Furthermore, if a taxpayer has made a tax return, then unless there has been fraudulent or negligent conduct on behalf of the taxpayer or somebody acting on his behalf, the Revenue is precluded from making a discovery after it has informed the taxpayer that it has completed its enquiries into the taxpayer's return. In the same way, if the period in which the Revenue could commence enquiries has expired, the Revenue cannot make a discovery unless it can show fraud or negligence. If an enquiry has been conducted into a taxpayer's return and the Revenue has issued notice that it has completed its enquiries, then the Revenue again is precluded from making a discovery (except for fraud or negligence), unless the discovery could not have been reasonably expected to have been made on the basis of the information available to the Revenue during the course of the enquiry.

For the purpose of the phrase 'information available to the officer', the Revenue is deemed to have such information available to it if:

(i) it is contained in a person's tax return, or in any accounts, statement or documents accompanying the return;

(ii) it is contained in any claim made by the taxpayer;

(iii) it is contained in any document, account or particulars which are produced to the Revenue for the purpose of the enquiry;

(iv) it has been provided to the Revenue in the above circumstances in either of the two immediately preceding returns; or

(v) it is information notified in writing by the taxpayer to the Revenue during the same period.

If the Revenue makes a discovery then penalties will arise under the existing legislation.

Penalty for late filing of tax return

5.14   It must be remembered that the tax return must be filed by 31 January, or three months after the date of issue. This is an absolute time limit and will result in a flat rate penalty of £100 if the filing date is missed. If the failure continues for a further six months the penalty will be increased by a further £100. The fixed penalties cannot exceed the tax liability for the year. If the tax return has not been filed one year after the filing date then the penalty is increased to the tax liability shown by the return. That penalty is appealable to the Commissioners.

In addition, the Revenue can apply to the Commissioners for a penalty of up to £60 per day for continued failure to file a tax return, but if this application is made before the second £100 penalty then that second penalty will not be applied.

The Commissioners can on appeal set aside the flat rate penalty if it appears to them that there is a reasonable excuse for the failure to file a tax return during the period of default. Similar penalties also apply to partnership returns.

Notification of chargeability

5.15   The penalty for failure to notify the chargeability by 6 October following the end of the fiscal year in which the income arises is a penalty of an amount up to the tax which remains unpaid as at 31 January following the year of assessment. This rule is introduced from 1995/96. It should be noted that in the case of a new business source notification will be required before the end of the first trading period in many instances.

Example

Jenny, who has part-time income, commenced trading on 1 November 1996. She makes her accounts up to 31 October 1996. The income first arose in the fiscal year 1996/97 and therefore the latest date for notification is 5 October 1997. The tax for 1996/97 is due on 31 January 1998, i.e. three months after the end of the accounting period.

The taxpayer may have to use a best estimate and correct that estimate when the true figure is known, with a charge to interest on any underpayment.

Keeping of records

5.16 To complement this brief review of penalties, it should be noted that all taxpayers must maintain such records as are necessary to complete their tax return for one year from 31 January following the end of the year of assessment. This period is increased if the return is filed late or amended to the anniversary of the quarter date of filing or of amendment. In the case of a person with income from self-employment or from letting of property the period becomes five years from 31 January following the year of assessment. The penalty for failure to retain records is an amount of up to £3,000. Records must also be maintained after the Revenue has commenced an enquiry until the completion of that enquiry.

Production of documents

5.17 If a taxpayer is under enquiry, then the Revenue may issue a notice requiring the production of documents that are in the taxpayer's power or possession. If the taxpayer fails to produce such documents as required by a notice then a penalty will be imposed. This will be a penalty of £50 together with a daily penalty for continued failure of an amount not exceeding £30 per day for each day the failure continues after the date on which the penalty of £50 is imposed. If the penalty is imposed by the Commissioners, the maximum amount is £150 per day.

Interest on penalties

5.18 Interest is payable upon late payment of penalties. Interest is charged from the date on which the penalty became due and payable until the date of payment.

Claims

5.19 Many time limits are altered by the introduction of self-assessment. The general rule becomes that a claim must be made by five years from 31 January following the end of the year of assessment. This is approximately nine weeks shorter than the present time limit of six years. This new general rule is introduced for 1996/97.

However, many claims are to be made in the new tax return. As that return must be complete and final by twelve months after 31 January following the end of the year of assessment, the normal time limit will become one year and ten months after the end of the fiscal year for many such claims.

Error or mistake claims

5.20 In the past it would have been possible to make an error or mistake claim. However, it is provided that error or mistake claims are specifically excluded where the claim should have been made in the tax return, and that for other allowable claims the time limit shall be five years from 31 January following the end of the year of assessment.

Error or mistake claims will not be allowed where a tax return has been completed on the basis of the practice generally prevailing at the time that the tax return was made.

Assessments for 1995/96 and earlier years

5.21 If an assessment to income tax or capital gains tax for 1995/96 or any earlier year is issued after 6 April 1998, then the interest and surcharge provisions of self-assessment will apply. This means that if a tax return was issued and completed for the earlier year by the due date (normally 31 October following the year of assessment) then if the Revenue issue an assessment for that earlier year after 6 April 1998 interest will run from 31 January following the end of the year of assessment. Taxpayers should therefore notify the Revenue of any unissued assessments in good time to enable such assessments to be issued by the Revenue before 6 April 1998 thereby avoiding the new interest charge. Interest in such circumstances would normally run from 30 days after the issue of the assessment.

Example

5.22 In 1994 Nigel sold farm land which was to be used for housing development giving rise to a capital gain of £500,000.

This was clearly shown upon the tax return to 5 April 1995 but the Inland Revenue did not assess.

In December 2000 the Revenue becomes aware that an assessment for 1994/95 capital gain has not been issued and issue an assessment on 3 January 2001 for £197,680 tax payable.

Because the assessment is for the year 1995/96 or earlier and was issued after 6 April 1998 then the rules of self-assessment apply. Interest therefore runs from 31 January following the end of the fiscal year, i.e. 31 January 1996. Furthermore if the tax remains unpaid 28 days after the normal due date then a surcharge will become due. The normal due date is 30 days after the issue of the notice of assessment, i.e. 2 February 2001 and the 5% surcharge would apply if the tax was unpaid by 2 March 2001. The surcharge would increase to 10% six months from the due date, i.e. 2 August 2001.

Penalties on employers

Forms P14 and P35

5.23 Automatic penalties are payable by employers who do not send in year end forms P14 and P35 by 19 May, or who send in incorrect returns. The penalty for failure to file by 19 May is £100 for every 50 employees (or part of 50) for each month or part of month the return is late. In addition interest is charged if PAYE and National Insurance contributions for any year to 5 April are paid later than 19 April.

Form P60

5.24 The form P60 is normally part of the P14 pack or its computer equivalent. Employers are required to give form P60 to employees working for them at 5 April not later than 31 May, e.g. for an employee on 5 April 1997 the form P60 must be given to that employee by 31 May 1997.

If an employer fails to provide the information to the employee by the deadline and the Inland Revenue becomes aware of that failure then it will remind the employer of his obligation and encourage compliance. The purpose of the new obligation is to enable employees to be able to complete their tax returns accurately and in good time. Providing the employer provides the information in such time that the employee can comply with his obligations to the Revenue then generally no penalty will be imposed by the Inland Revenue on the employer. However, if the employer persists in failing to comply or the amount of tax involved is significant then the Inland Revenue will consider imposing a penalty of up to £300 per form. This penalty is imposed by the General or Special Commissioners. The Commissioners can order a further penalty of up to £60 per form per day that the failure continues.

The Revenue will not generally consider taking any action to recover penalties unless an employee tells them of an employer's failure.

Forms P11D and P9D

5.25   An employer is obliged to file a form P11D or form P9D for each employee for whom benefits have been provided or expense payments made by 6 July. In addition the employer will be required to give the employee a copy of the relevant form P11D or P9D.

Failure to file by the due date can give rise to an initial penalty of up to £300 per form imposed by the General or Special Commissioners together with a further penalty of up to £60 per form for each day that the failure continues. These are the maximum sums of penalty covering a wide range of circumstances and the Revenue does not normally ask the Commissioners to impose the maximum penalty. However, if a form is not filed by the due date and the case is listed for hearing before the Commissioners, then even if the breach has been remedied before the hearing, i.e. the relevant forms filed, it is still possible for the Revenue to continue with the hearing and to ask for a penalty to be imposed for late filing.

Where the Inland Revenue discovers that an employer has provided incomplete information or that forms P11D or P9D contain errors, then it will normally ask the employer to provide an explanation of the error before penalty action is considered. If the employer can show that the error or omission is entirely innocent no penalty will arise. Therefore a genuine mistake made in good faith, e.g. in the calculation of a figure shown on the form will not give rise to a penalty.

In practice the Inland Revenue pursues very few P11D/P9D penalties to the Commissioners instead preferring to arrange voluntary settlements with the employer to collect any tax and National Insurance due. Where the form P11D or P9D is incorrect or incomplete there is a maximum penalty of £3,000 per form.

In addition to completing the form P11D or P9D and forwarding the same to the Revenue by 6 July the employer will also have to provide a copy of the form P11D to his employees. He will be obliged to provide a form to all employees in service on 5 April. In the case of employees who have left since that date the form may be sent to the last known address. If the employer fails to provide a copy of the form P11D or P9D to the employee then the Revenue can ask the Commissioners to impose the same penalty on the employer as for failure to file the form with the Revenue, i.e. up to £300 per form plus a further penalty of up to £60 per day. However, it will be the policy of the Inland Revenue not to ask for penalties initially, but to remind the employer of his obligations and to encourage compliance. Penalties will only be imposed where the failure persists or the amount of tax involved is significant.

An employer does not automatically have to give a copy of form P11D or P9D to employees who left during the tax year. However, if such an employee requires a copy of the form then the employer must provide the information within 30 days of the written request or 6 July following the end of the relevant tax year if later. The employee is only allowed to make one written request. Again failure to comply can result in the General or Special Commissioners imposing a penalty of up to £300 per form together with a daily penalty of up to £60 per form. In practice the Revenue will encourage compliance rather than automatically apply for a penalty.

Third parties

5.26   A third party providing a benefit to an employee is required to provide written details of that benefit including its cash equivalent value to the employee by 6 July following the end of the tax year.

This requirement does not normally involve the Inland Revenue. If an employee does not receive such notification and informs the Inland Revenue of the failure then the Revenue will contact the third party to persuade it to comply with its obligation. Only in the last resort will the Inland Revenue consider taking the matter to the General or Special Commissioners for the penalty of £300 per form together with up to £60 per day for continued failure.

Although the Inland Revenue can also require the third party to make returns of such benefits directly to them this will not be done automatically. If the third party fails to comply with the notice then the Revenue can apply to the Commissioners for the usual penalty of up to £300 per form and a continuing penalty of up to £60 per day. For an incorrect or fraudulent return the penalty is up to £3,000 per return.

Chapter 6

Payments of Tax for 1996/97

Payments on account in 1996/97

6.1   Under the new self-assessment provisions the taxpayer is required to make payments on account of tax on 31 January in the year of assessment and 31 July following the end of the year of assessment. These amounts are normally based upon the tax assessed for the preceding year, after deduction of tax paid at source, PAYE, tax credits and SC60 tax. A final settling up payment is then due on 31 January following the end of the year of assessment. That payment will include the capital gains liability.

6.2   The new provisions are introduced with effect from 1996/97 (for partnerships the new rules apply from 1997/98). However, the first self-assessment tax return will not be issued until 1996/97 i.e. on 5 April 1997. Therefore special rules are needed to calculate the payment on account in 1996/97. As the taxpayer will not have information on hand for 1995/96 the Revenue will calculate the payment on account and will issue payment demands in the normal way.

Employees

6.3   Most employees do not pay tax by assessment and accordingly will be unaffected by the new rules. PAYE will continue to be deducted and any underpayments calculated and coded in to future years' code number. Even where a tax return is issued to an employed person it is not the Revenue practice to demand tax for small amounts. Instead such amounts are collected by reducing the code number. If the reduction exceeds the available allowances then a K code is issued increasing the tax deduction from employment.

Under the new proposals the system will continue with underpayments of less than £1,000 being coded in in this way. Therefore most employees will not be required to make payments on account.

Because an employee will need his coding notice to compute the tax payable under the self-assessment system it is essential that employees realise that the coding notice for 1996/97 must be kept. The first such coding notices will be issued late 1995 or early 1996. The relevant information on the code notice will be the underpayments for 1994/95 coded into the 1996/97 notice. It is also possible that there will be amendments to the 1995/96 code notice which again will give rise to an underpayment in 1995/96 that will be collected in 1996/97.

Where an employer receives a revised code notice for 1996/97 that should also be retained as it could show an underpayment for 1996/97 that will be collected in 1997/98. Such an amount will be deducted from the liability for 1996/97 in arriving at the balancing payment due on 31 January 1998.

Higher rate tax on investment income

6.4   Where a taxpayer has investment income liable to higher rate tax, and the amount cannot be coded in as mentioned above, then the Revenue currently issues a demand, payable on 1 December following the end of the fiscal year. Under self-assessment the higher rate tax liability will be collected by inclusion within the payment upon account system with any balancing payment/repayment occurring 31 January following the end of the year of assessment.

For 1996/97 higher rate liability is not included in the new system. Accordingly a demand will not be issued for a payment on 1 December 1997. Instead the amount will be included in the first self-assessment and the full liability will be payable on 31 January 1998. It must be remembered that the liability for 1997/98 payments on account will be based upon the 1996/97 liability including higher rate on investment income. Accordingly a payment on account will be required on 31 January 1998 equal to one-half of the assessable income for 1996/97. The effect is therefore that 150% of the higher rate liability on investment income is payable on 31 January 1998, and thereafter the liability arises half yearly.

Income from land, untaxed interest and overseas income

6.5   Previously tax assessed under these headings was payable on 1 January in the year of assessment. Under self-assessment tax is payable half yearly on 31 January and 31 July.

For 1996/97 the Revenue will issue a demand payable on 31 January 1997 for an amount equal to the 1995/96 liability. Any additional amounts payable or repayable will be due on 31 January 1998.

For 1997/98 a payment on account will be due on 31 January 1998 as to one-half and 31 July 1998 as to one-half. These will be based upon the previous year's liability with a balancing adjustment on 31 January 1999.

Income from trades, professions and vocations (other than partnerships)

6.6 Previously tax was payable in two equal half yearly instalments on 1 January and 1 July. Under self-assessment tax continues to be payable in the same but on 31 January and 31 July.

The payment on account for 1996/97 will be based upon the agreed assessment for the year 1995/96. Note that under self-assessment that liability is not recomputed for changes in rates or allowances in the following year. Therefore the amount payable on 31 January 1997 will equal the amount paid on 1 January 1996. In the same way the amount payable on 31 July 1997 will equal the amount paid on 1 July 1996. For this purpose income tax includes Class 4 National Insurance payments.

The 1996/97 liability will be calculated on the tax return issued on or after 6 April 1997 and any balancing adjustment will be paid or repaid on 31 January 1998.

Reductions of payment on account

6.7 Where the payment on account in 1996/97 is likely to be excessive the taxpayer may make a claim to reduce the amount payable if he has reasonable grounds for believing that the liability is overstated. However, if the payment on account is reduced and it subsequently proves that it should not have been reduced then interest will be payable on the reduction from the normal due date for payment to the actual date of payment.

Partnerships

6.8 Assessments for 1996/97 will be issued by the Revenue on an estimated basis. The normal appeal and postponement procedures will apply with the first instalment of tax being due by the partnership on 1 January 1997 and the second instalment on 1 July 1997. The partnership will file a partnership statement and return. Each partner will then file a self-assessment tax return before 31 January 1998 paying the balance of any tax due. The tax paid by the partnership on behalf of the partners will be treated as tax deducted at source by the individual partners. Note if a partner has other income liable to assessment then payments on account in 1996/97 will be required on 31 January and 31 July 1997 in the normal way.

Example

6.9   Jenny, who is single, has income from employment in 1995/96 of £20,350 on which PAYE of £4,046 was deducted. She receives a code notice for 1996/97 showing:

	£		£
Personal allowances	3,525	Underpaid tax 1994/95 of £300	1,200
		Net allowances	2,325

1996/97 Code No 232L

On 1 November 1996 she is provided with a company car and fuel on which the taxable benefit in 1996/97 is £1,465. Her code number is altered from March 1997 to 86L month one basis and underpaid tax of £1,172 @ 25% = £293 (i.e. from November 1996 to February 1997) is to be collected by way of code number adjustment in 1997/98. Her P60 for 1996/97 shows pay £22,000, tax deducted £4,788. Her P11D shows a cash equivalent for car and fuel of £1,465.

In addition Jenny has the following income and gains:

	1995/96 £	1996/97 £
National savings bank	4,200	4,800
(Amount received in 1994/95 = £4,000)		
Dividends (net)	2,800	3,200
Building society interest received (net)	3,000	3,600
Capital gains	9,000	6,600

Her tax liabilities will be payable as follows:

1995/96		£	Tax Paid
Employment		20,350	4,046
National savings bank (preceding year basis)		4,000	1,000
Tax paid thereon on 1 January 1996			
Dividends	2,800		
Tax credits @ 20%	700	3,500	700

	£	£	Tax Paid
Building society interest	3,000		
Tax deducted @ 25%	1,000	4,000	1,000
		31,850	6,746
Less personal allowance		3,525	
		28,325	
Income tax			
3,200 @ 20%		640	
21,100 @ 25%		5,275	
4,025 @ 40%		1,610	7,525
			779

being higher rate tax due on investment income of

Dividends		3,500	
Building society interest (balance)		525	
		4,025 @ 40% = 1,610	

Less tax credits			
Dividends	20% x 3,500	700	
Building society 25% x	525	131	831

Tax payable on 1 December 1996			779

Capital gains

Gain		9,000	
Less annual exemption		6,000	
Payable 1 December 1996		3,000 @ 40%	1,200

1996/97
Payments on account
31 January 1997 (being amount payable 1 January 1996)

National savings bank interest	1,000

31 July 1997 (being amount payable 1 July 1996)   Nil

31 January 1998 (being balance of tax due for 1996/97
                  plus payment on account for 1997/98)

Employment per P60		22,000
Benefit in kind per P11D		1,465
National savings bank (transitional year)		
1/2 (4,200 + 4,800)		4,500
Dividends	3,200	
Tax credits @ 20%	800	4,000
Building society interest	3,600	
Tax deducted @ 25%	1,200	4,800

57

6.9 *Payments of Tax for 1996/97*

	£	Tax Paid
	36,765	
<u>Less</u> personal allowance	<u>3,525</u>	
	33,240	

Income tax
3,200 @ 20%	640	
21,100 @ 25%	5,275	
8,940 @ 40%	<u>3,576</u>	
	9,491	

Capital gains
Gain	6,600	
<u>Less</u> annual exemption	6,000	
	600	@ 40% = <u>240</u>

Computation of tax due 31 January 1998

Income tax due	9,491	
Capital gains tax due	<u>240</u>	
	9,731	
Underpaid tax 1994/95	<u>300</u>	10,031

Payments made in 1996/97
PAYE	4,788	
Payments on account – 31 January 1997	1,000	
– 31 July 1997	–	
Tax credits	800	
Tax deducted at source	<u>1,200</u>	<u>7,788</u>

Tax due for 1996/97		2,243
Amount to be collected by PAYE		
Coding adjustment in 1997/98		<u>293</u>
Payment for 1996/97 due 31 January 1998		1,950

Payment on account 1997/98
Amount due for 1996/97	1,950	
Payments made on account in 1996/97	<u>1,000</u>	
	2,950	
<u>Less</u> capital gains tax	<u>240</u>	
50% thereof	<u>2,710</u>	1,355
Tax payable on 31 January 1998		<u>3,305</u>

Payment on account due 31 July 1998		
(being remaining 50% of £2,710)		<u>1,355</u>

Chapter 7

Current Year Basis of Assessment

Preceding year basis — the reasons for change

7.1 The reforms introduced by the *Finance Act 1994* rank as amongst the most fundamental changes this century in the way in which individuals deal with their taxation affairs. Not only does the onus for the computation of the tax liability due move from the Inland Revenue to the taxpayer but also the basis of computation of taxable income for many sources is changed.

Under the current system, income from trades, professions and vocations together with income from investments not taxed at source and income from securities and possessions outside the United Kingdom were taxed on a preceding year basis.

The use of preceding year basis meant that the assessable profits in opening years had to be calculated under a formula, and that in closing years there was a period of time for which the profits earned never effectively formed the basis of an assessment. The complexity and inequity of the system together with exploitation of the opening and closing year rules led the Government to introduce changes whereby the amount that will be taxed is normally the amount of income arising.

Current year basis — the concepts

7.2 From 6 April 1994 for new sources and from 6 April 1997 for existing sources income will be assessed for trades, professions, vocations, untaxed investment income and overseas income on a current year basis.

In the case of income other than profits from a trade or profession, etc. the income to be taxed will be that which arises during the fiscal year.

For businesses the profits to be taxed will be those for the accounts that end in the fiscal year. Therefore if a business man makes up his accounts for the year to 31 August 1999 these will be treated as forming the basis of the assessment for the fiscal year 1999/2000.

For the year 1996/97 for existing sources there will be transitional provisions. In the case of investment income and overseas income the assessment will be based upon one-half of the sum of the income arising during 1995/96 and 1996/97. In the case of businesses, the assessment will be based upon one-half of the adjusted income for the accounts that end in the years 1995/96 and 1996/97. The principles are outlined in 7.3 below but for greater detail see Tolley's *Guide to Self-Assessment for the Self-Employed.*

Special rules apply to sources of income that cease before 5 April 1998, or businesses that cease before 5 April 1999.

Income from trades, etc — Schedule DI and II

7.3   The current year basis of assessment for businesses enables the trader to choose a year end that is most convenient for the business. It is the intention of the legislation to ensure that no advantage or material disadvantage arises from the use of any given accounting date. Furthermore, a trader may change his accounting date at any time. The Revenue must be notified within twelve months of 31 January following the end of the fiscal year of change. Furthermore if a trader has changed his accounting date within the previous five years the Revenue must give permission for the change of accounting date.

The most important change introduced by the current year rules is that the profits of the business will be assessed once only. Under the previous preceding year basis there was a doubling up of profits at the beginning of a business followed by a gap period on cessation. The previous system therefore did not give a perfect match between assessments and earnings. The new system will ensure that the exact profits earned are assessed over the life of the business, however, there will still be timing differences, and because tax rates may vary, there will still be different overall tax liabilities depending upon the accounting date chosen.

For simplicity and accuracy an accounting date of 5 April will always give an exact match between profits earned and those assessed. In practice the Revenue will also accept 31 March as being co-terminous with 5 April giving the same end result.

Where any other accounting date is chosen, special rules will apply in opening and closing years.

If a business lasts less than two fiscal, actual basis will apply throughout.

7.4   Summary of basis of assessment – opening years

Year of Assessment	Basis of Assessment
Year of commencement	Profits from commencement to following 5 April
Second year of trading — where accounts are prepared to a date ending in the second year for a period of:	
— under twelve months	Profits of the first twelve months from date of commencement
— twelve months or more	Profits for the year ending on the accounting date
— no accounts ending in the year	Profits for the year ended 5 April (i.e. actual)
Third year of trading	Profits for the accounts ending on the accounting date

Where the above rules mean that profits are taken into account more than once then the duplicated amount forms the basis of a relief known as overlap relief. It is necessary to compute the actual amount that overlaps and the number of days in the overlap period. Credit for this relief will be given for such profits, without indexation, when the business ceases, or, if the accounting date is changed resulting in an assessment for a period in excess of twelve months. Relief is given for the number of days assessed in excess of one year.

Existing businesses

7.5   1995/96 will be the last year to which the old preceding year rules apply.

1996/97 will be a transitional year with assessment being based on 365-day part of the profits from the end of the accounts used for the 1995/96 base period to the beginning of the base period for 1997/98.

1997/98 will be the first year to which the current year basis of assessment applies.

7.6   *Current Year Basis of Assessment*

Example

Malcolm has always made his accounts up to 30 June. His basis periods during the transitional period will be as follows:

1995/96 — Preceding year basis
Assessment based upon the adjusted profits for the year ended 30 June 1994.

1996/97 — Transitional year
Profits based upon 365 days out of 731 days of the period.

365 days to 30 June 1995
<u>366</u> days to 30 June 1996
<u>731</u>

1997/98 — Current year basis
Profits for this year will be based upon the year ended 30 June 1997, i.e. the accounts ending in the year of assessment.

Overlap relief — existing businesses

7.6   Insofar as the assessment of an existing business relates to the period before 6 April 1997 for the year 1997/98 then overlap relief will be given. This relief is computed on the adjusted profits for 1997/98 before deducting capital allowances. Normally all current year assessments are based upon profits after capital allowances. Again the relief will only be given when the business ceases, or changes its accounting date such that it is assessed on a period of more than twelve months.

Assessments when a business ceases

7.7   Normally a business is assessed upon the profits from the end of the accounts in the previous fiscal year to the accounting date in the current fiscal year. This means that if accounts are made up to a consistent date each year the assessment will be based upon a twelve-month period. The same principle will apply when a business ceases. That is to say that the amount to be taken into account will be the profits from the accounting date used for the preceding year to the date of cessation. If more than one set of accounts end in the year of cessation then the earlier accounting date is ignored. This means that up to 23 months three weeks profits can be assessed in the final year. This excessive assessment is reduced by the overlap relief that was created when the business commenced, or moved into current year basis in 1997/98. Nevertheless if an accounting date of other than 31 March/5 April is used this can give rise to an excessive assessment on cessation.

Example

Malcolm, who makes his accounts to 30 June, ceases on 1 February 2000. His assessments will be:

1998/99 — Current year basis
Profits for the year ended 30 June 1998

1999/2000 — Final year
Assessment based upon profits from the date used for the preceding year to date of cessation i.e.

Profits at the year ended 30 June 1999 +
Profits of the period 1 July 1999 to 1 February 2000

The above assessment is reduced by the overlap relief calculated in 1997/98.

Businesses ceasing before 5 April 1999

7.8   If a business ceases before 6 April 1997 and had commenced before 6 April 1994 then the old preceding year basis rules apply.

If a business that had commenced before 6 April 1994 ceases in the year 1997/98 then the Inland Revenue may elect that the new rules do not apply, i.e. the assessments are computed totally under the preceding year rules.

Where a businesses finishes in the fiscal year 1998/99 then the current year rules with the transitional relief explained above apply. However, for businesses that commenced before 6 April 1994 the Revenue will elect to assess in the year 1996/97 the higher of the transitional profits or the actual profits for that year.

Anti-avoidance

7.9   To prevent profits being moved from a period of time assessed in full to the transitional year, or to the first year assessed on the current year basis where overlap relief will be available, anti-avoidance provisions are introduced. The provisions may also apply where a change of accounting date occurs, however, the rules will not apply if the accounting date is moved closer to 5 April 1997.

The effect of the anti-avoidance rules will be to penalise the taxpayer by an amount equal to 25% of the profits on which it was attempted to avoid tax.

Chapter 8

Partnerships

Self-assessment with partnership income

8.1   The legislation introduced by the *Finance Acts 1994* and *1995* makes fundamental and far-reaching changes to the taxation of partnerships. Previously it was provided that where two or more persons carried on a trade or profession the income tax was computed for the partnership and they were jointly liable for that tax.

For partnerships:

(*a*)   commencing on or after 6 April 1994;

(*b*)   changing partners after 6 April 1994 and not making a continuation election;

(*c*)   existing from 1997/98;

then the partnership will no longer be assessed to tax in its own name. Instead each individual partner will be responsible for his own taxation liability.

Division of income between the partners

8.2   Notwithstanding the fact that the partnership is not assessed to tax the income of the partnership will still be computed in accordance with the Schedules to arrive at the taxable amount. That amount will then be divided between the partners in the profit sharing ratio of the period. If the partnership chooses an accounting date other than 5 April then the accounts must be prepared for all untaxed sources of income for the same period.

Example

A & B are in partnership preparing accounts to 30 June 1999. They receive income from letting of property. The Schedule A income from letting computation must be prepared for the year ended 30 June 1999.

If the partnership also has taxed income such as income from employment included as part of the partnership profits (e.g. a partnership of doctors where one doctor holds a hospital appointment) then that income must be included in the partnership statement for the year to 5 April.

Example

In A & B (above) the trading income and letting income would be for the year to 30 June 1999 whereas the income from employment and dividend income would be for the year to 5 April 2000. The income and any relevant tax attached thereto is then divided between the partners in the partnership profit sharing ratio of the relevant period, i.e. for trading income, lettings, etc. for the year to 30 June 1999 and for employment and dividends in the above example for the year to 5 April 2000.

Overlap relief

8.3   Where a partnership uses an accounting date of other than 31 March/5 April then overlap relief will apply. In the case of trading profits this is computed as for individuals, see Chapter 7 above. The resultant overlap relief is divided between the individual partners in accordance with his profit sharing ratio for the period of overlap. Each individual partner can use the relief when he ceases to be a partner in the business. Relief will also be given if the partnership changes its accounting date by moving nearer to 5 April.

Where a partnership has other untaxed income then all such income, from whatever source, will be the deemed income of a second deemed trade. Overlap relief will be calculated as though the income arose from a trade. It will then be divided between the partners in accordance with the profit sharing ratio of the period of overlap. The relief will be claimable by the individual partner when they cease to be a member of the partnership, or where the partnership changes its accounting date. It should be noted that no relief will be given where the source of income ceases. Because the relief may arise in a year when there is no income from the second deemed source any surplus relief will be given against other income in the year of cessation.

8.4   The partnership is responsible for making a return of the income to the Revenue showing the division of the income between the partners. This is known as a partnership statement. The partners must also make a partnership return showing the name, address and tax reference number of each partner. It will be usual for a partnership to nominate one partner to be responsible for providing the above information to the Inland Revenue.

The time limit for filing the partnership return and the partnership statement will be 31 January following the end of the year of assessment. However, in practice it will be necessary to complete and file the partnership return and statement well before that date to enable the partnership to provide the individual partners with details of the income from relevant sources and tax credits available to include in his own personal return. Each individual partner will be responsible for his own tax return and paying his own share of tax. They are also each responsible for ensuring that the partnership returns are filed on time.

If the individual partner does not receive details of his share of income in time to complete his own tax return because the partnership returns have not been filed on time then there will be a penalty. This penalty is collected from the individual in respect of the failure to file his own tax return together with a further penalty in respect of failure to file a partnership return, i.e. there will be a double penalty.

Chapter 9

Other Changes

Principles of self-assessment

9.1 The introduction of self-assessment and the current year basis will have a far-reaching effect on the way all taxes are assessed and collected.

The basic principle of calculating the liability to tax by reference to the rules of a Schedule continues to apply. Having arrived at the quantum of the assessable income then those amounts are aggregated to form one self-assessment.

Because the taxpayer is making a self-assessment, he will only deal with one tax office and he will only have one tax reference.

Income from land — Schedule A

9.2 From 6 April 1995 all income of an individual from UK land including amounts receivable for the use of furniture is treated as income from a single business. The basis of assessment is always the fiscal year. Accordingly income from unfurnished lettings, furnished lettings, fixed caravans and permanently moored houseboats and other payments in respect of land are all combined. The source is treated as a business and expenses are deducted in accordance with the normal accountancy rules for businesses. The resultant net profit is included in the self-assessment. However, any losses cannot be offset against other income. They will be carried forward and relieved against future income from land. Any unrelieved losses at 5 April 1995 arising from land, including unrelieved interest on property loans, will be aggregated and relieved against property income.

Furnished holiday lettings will continue to be treated as a deemed trade, but assessable under Schedule A. This means that statements of income and expenses for furnished holiday lettings must be prepared for the year to 5 April in all instances from 1995/96 onwards. Losses will continue to be available for offset against other income.

9.3 *Other Changes*

Untaxed interest — Schedule D Case III

9.3   The basis of assessment of untaxed interest and other Schedule D Case III income changes from preceding year basis (in most instances) to an actual basis on all occasions except when received by a partnership. The new provisions apply to new sources from 6 April 1994. In the case of existing sources the old rules apply if the source ceases before 6 April 1998.

9.4   In the case of continuing sources, that is to say, where the income arose before 6 April 1994 and continues beyond 5 April 1998, then:

(*a*)   the old rules apply for 1994/95 and 1995/96 (preceding year basis);

(*b*)   for 1996/97, the assessment will be one-half of the sum of the interest received in 1995/96 and 1996/97; and

(*c*)   for 1997/98 and subsequent years, the income actually arising in the fiscal year will form the basis of assessment.

It must be remembered that if the old rules apply, i.e. there is a cessation before 6 April 1998, then the Revenue has the option to revise the penultimate assessment to actual.

Example of a continuing source

9.5   Henry Ing has received bank deposit interest for many years. His interest received is:

		£
Year ended 5 April 1995		1,800
5 April 1996		1,750
5 April 1997		1,650
5 April 1998		1,500

His income assessable under Schedule D Case III is:

		£
1995/96 (preceding year basis)		1,800
1996/97 (transitional year)		
Year ended 5 April 1996	1,750	
Year ended 5 April 1997	1,650	
50% x	3,400	1,700
1997/98 (actual)		1,500

70

Example of a source closing before 5 April 1998

9.6   Henry closes his deposit account on 31 December 1997, with interest for that part year of £1,500.

His assessable Schedule D Case III income would be:

	£
1995/96 (preceding year basis)	1,800
1996/97 (preceding year basis)	1,750
(with Revenue option to revise	
to actual — £1,650)	
1997/98 (actual)	1,500

(The transitional year (1996/97) only applies if the source continues beyond 5 April 1998.)

Example of a new source

9.7   Ingrid James opened a National Savings investment account in June 1994.

Her income from that account was:

	£
Year ended 5 April 1995	1,800
5 April 1996	1,750
5 April 1997	1,650
5 April 1998	1,500

Her Schedule D Case III assessments are all on an actual basis:

	£
1994/95	1,800
1995/96	1,750
1996/97	1,650
1997/98	1,500

Overseas income — Schedule D Cases IV and V

9.8   Similar rules apply to overseas income as to UK income. If the source is a foreign trade, profession or vocation chargeable to tax under Schedule D Case IV or Case V, it is to be assessed as though it were a Schedule D Case I source (see 7.3 above onwards).

9.9 *Other Changes*

That is to say, in future years the current year basis of assessment will apply, with transitional rules for 1996/97 and overlap relief as for Schedule D Cases I and II.

Other sources of Schedule D Case IV and Case V income are to be treated as for Schedule D Case III above, that is to say on an actual basis providing the source continues beyond 5 April 1998.

9.9 Summary of basis of assessment

If source arises before 6 April 1994 and continues beyond 5 April 1998	Actual basis applies for 1997/98 onwards
	Transitional rules apply for 1996/97, that is one-half of the income arising in 1995/96 and 1996/97
	Preceding year basis applies up to and including 1995/96. If 1995/96 is on actual basis, then actual will apply throughout
If source commences after 5 April 1994	New rules apply 1994 immediately (actual basis)
If source ceases before 6 April 1998 and had commenced before 6 April 1994	Preceding year basis rules apply throughout

Remittance basis

9.10 Because the remittance basis may apply to Schedule D Cases IV and V, anti-avoidance provisions have been introduced in the *Finance Act 1995* to prevent exceptionally large remittances being made during the transitional period. Without such provisions, it would have been possible to make large remittances during the period 6 April 1995 to 5 April 1997 and only 50% thereof would be taxed.

Other income — Schedule D Case VI

9.11 Income tax under Schedule D Case VI will be computed on the full amount of profits or gains arising in the year of assessment. This applies immediately to sources of Schedule D Case VI income arising on or after 6 April 1994 and to existing sources with effect from 1996/97.

In practice, Schedule D Case VI is often dealt with on an accounts basis or even on a preceding year basis. It is expected that the Revenue will allow a current year basis to apply in the future to those sources already dealt with on that basis. This will apply automatically to partnerships.

In the case of Schedule D Case VI currently being assessed on a preceding year basis, it is expected that transitional provisions will apply for 1996/97 by taking 50% of the income that would have been assessed for that year on the preceding year basis, i.e. 1995/96 plus the current year income, i.e. that arriving in 1996/97.

Capital gains

9.12 The taxpayer must include details of capital gains and capital losses within the tax return. Any capital gains tax payable will be due on 31 January following the end of the year of assessment. Under self-assessment the taxpayer must make a claim for capital losses within the tax return. If a claim is not made then loss relief will not be granted. The legislation provides that losses of 1996/97 and subsequent years are to be deductible from capital gains in preference to capital losses of earlier years brought forward.

In computing a capital gain or capital loss it is necessary in many instances to use a valuation. Valuations necessarily require the exercise of judgement, and more than one figure may equally be sustainable. The basis of valuation should be shown in the tax return. If the taxpayer believes that the valuation is a considered figure then it will be regarded as the final figure subject to the Revenue's right to enquire into the tax return. If the Revenue does not enquire into a valuation figure within the normal enquiry period, i.e. within twelve months of 31 January following the end of the year of assessment (or later if the return is filed later), then it cannot challenge that valuation at a later date unless it is 'unreasonable'.

If the taxpayer believes that the figure is an estimate then it should be shown as such on the return and the figure should be corrected as soon as any missing information is reasonably available.

The Inland Revenue intends to issue a more detailed statement on estimates and valuations before 1997.

Future legislation

9.13 The Inland Revenue is currently undertaking further consultation with interested parties and this will result in further legislation, to be included in the Finance Act 1996, in respect of self-assessment and the current year basis.

It is to be expected that there will be numerous changes to detailed points relating to self-assessment and the current year basis in many of the forthcoming Finance Bills. As many provisions do not come into force until 1996/97 or 1997/98, it is essential to refer to such legislation when available before giving definitive advice.

Index

Tolley's
Tax Reference Annuals
1995-96

With each new edition the standard of excellence established in **Tolley's Tax Reference Annuals** over the past seventy-nine years is not simply maintained but consistently improved. Every year our experienced in-house authors edit and revise the annuals to ensure that you have the most up-to-date tax commentary available. This year, following extensive market research, major changes and improvements have been made to the 1995-96 editions:

- More than 200 additional worked examples
- Expanded to include references to the Inland Revenue's Internal Guidance Manuals for the first time
- Inclusion of newly reported Special Commissioners' decisions
- Improved indexes
- A complete overhaul of the VAT annual to take account of the VAT Act 1994

The collective result is a concise set of reference works expressly designed to keep the user fully up-to-date with the minimum of effort.

Tolley's Income Tax 1995-96
Glyn Saunders MA, David Smailes FCA

July 1995	950pp approx	**Order Code IT95**
ISBN 1 86012 008-3		**£32.95**

Tolley's Corporation Tax 1995-96
Glyn Saunders MA, Alan Dolton MA(Oxon)

July 1995	550pp approx	**Order Code CT95**
ISBN 1 86012 011-3		**£28.95**

Tolley's Capital Gains Tax 1995-96
Patrick Noakes MA FCA ATII, Gary B Mackley-Smith FFA FIAB AIMgt

July 1995	650pp approx	**Order Code CGT95**
ISBN 1 86012 010-5		**£29.95**

Tolley's Inheritance Tax 1995-96
Patrick Noakes MA FCA ATII, Jon Golding ATT

July 1995	300pp approx	**Order Code IHT95**
ISBN 1 86012 009-1		**£25.95**

Tolley's Value Added Tax 1995-96
Robert Wareham BSc(Econ) FCA

July 1995	760pp approx	**Order Code VAT95**
ISBN 1 86012 012-1		**£28.95**

Tolley's National Insurance Contributions 1995-96
From an original text by Neil D Booth FCA FTII
Edited by Jon Golding ATT with consulting editors, KPMG, Employee Issues Group Leeds

June 1995	500pp approx	**Order Code NIC95**
ISBN 1 86012 013-X		**£33.95**

ORDERS AND ENQUIRIES

To Tolley's Customer Services Department at Tolley Publishing Co. Ltd., FREEPOST, 2 Addiscombe Road, Croydon, Surrey, CR9 5WZ.
Telephone: 0181-686 9141 Fax: 0181-686 3155.

Tolley

Remember, all Tolley publications are available on 21 days' approval.